THE BREEDING AND REARING OF DOGS

By the same author

THE ANATOMY OF DOG BREEDING
THE CONFORMATION OF THE DOG
WHAT MAKES A GOOD HORSE
THE MIND OF THE DOG
HOW ANIMALS TALK
THE FEMALE OF THE SPECIES
ANIMAL VISION
VETERINARY OPHTHALMOLOGY
CLINICAL VETERINARY SURGERY (two vols)
THE EXAMINATION OF ANIMALS FOR SOUNDNESS
HORSES IN ACTION
THE MIND OF THE HORSE
THE HORSE: STRUCTURE AND MOVEMENT
EXCUSE MY TAIL
THE HAUNTS AND HABITS OF FISHES
THE PRIVATE LIFE OF THE DOG
THE DOG: STRUCTURE AND MOVEMENT
HEALERS ON HORSEBACK
ANIMAL PSYCHOLOGY

THE BREEDING AND REARING OF DOGS

R. H. Smythe

Illustrated by the author

ARCO PUBLISHING COMPANY, INC.
New York

Published in the United States
by ARCO PUBLISHING COMPANY, Inc.
219 Park Avenue South, New York, N.Y. 10003

Library of Congress Catalogue Number 72-92618

Standard Book Number 668-02063-6

Printed in Great Britain

CONTENTS

ILLUSTRATIONS IN THE TEXT

Author's Introduction

This volume is intended primarily for the breeder and all who are interested in rearing puppies. The range of information it contains is so wide, however, that it will be of considerable value to everyone who owns a dog, or contemplates doing so.

It began as a reprint, with additions, of a number of articles by the same author that have appeared during the past few years in *Our Dogs*, but these have been amplified and supplemented and rearranged in chapters, with a comprehensive index that will permit the dog owner to look up any matter in which he may be particularly interested in the least possible time.

Since it is unlikely that many readers will find time to read the book through at one sitting, a slight amount of repetition may creep in, but this is unavoidable, since, without it, each separate section might not be clear unless one read other chapters as well. The present arrangement enables the reader to obtain full information regarding various subjects simply by looking up the index and reading the appropriate chapter.

The author is indebted to Dennis Marples, Esq., editor of *Our Dogs*, for permission to reprint a great many of the articles that form the basis of this volume, and also to his friend Commander T. Norman Hinton, for selecting material he thought might prove most valuable to the breeder and dog owner.

R.H.S.

I

The Brood Bitch

The success of every dog-breeding project centres primarily around the brood bitch. It is desirable to breed strong healthy puppies but it is also necessary for those destined for exhibition to grow into sound animals and to conform with the requirements of an approved standard.

It might be imagined by those who have little experience in dog breeding that all that would be necessary would be to mate a champion bitch with a champion dog of the same species in order to produce a champion litter.

Such is far from being the case, except by a lucky chance, since to produce puppies very like themselves the blood lines of sire and dam have, as breeders say, to 'nick', which in other words means that each carries genes complementary to the other, a not very common occurrence.

It is true that some kennels contrive to turn out a champion each year, but they are usually those that contain a number of bitches often similarly bred, and their owners have been fortunate enough to discover a sire that 'nicks', and they are sensible enough to continue for so long as may appear advisable to use the same blood lines. Even then the proportion of puppies that grow into dogs and bitches capable of holding their own in championship shows is not very high and one might well need to produce a considerable number of litters each year to enjoy any prospect of breeding one specimen capable of winning challenge certificates.

Regarding breeding, as it is carried out on general lines rather than by established breeders, brood bitches capable of producing puppies that grow well and conform with the standard are by no means always those that have been most successful in the ring, but they are sound, active and intelligent, usually with good pedigrees behind them. Many of them possess some minor fault or faults, a small percentage of which will be passed on to their puppies, but certain good features, such as excellent necks and shoulders, good ribs and the right type of bone, are likely to be passed on also. They should be easy whelpers, good mothers, and possess excellent temperaments. It is true, of course, that the tendency today, now that shows are so plentiful, is to make greater use of winning dams, but in days gone by less attention was paid to the female side and far more to the sire. A winning sire, and particularly one with the requisite number of challenge certificates, will be unlikely to possess many undesirable features in conformation, but his intelligence may or may not be up to standard.

The urgent need to introduce or preserve show points may induce the breeder to overlook temperament and intelligence and to produce certain litters that grow up with good conformation but possess a very low intelligence quotient, or nervous or untrustworthy dispositions. It is wise never to use such dogs as sires, and it is possible, when line breeding is aimed at, that they may have near relations not quite so close to the standard as regards conformation but with better temperaments and greater intelligence. One often produces better puppies from a near relative of the champion than from the champion himself.

Years ago it was regarded as essential to look for quality in the male, for strength and soundness in the female, and for correct temperament in both. Today most breeders realise that these qualities should exist in both scxes, but many are apt to pay too little regard to temperament. One has always to bear in mind that one is not trying to produce a *normal* representative of a particular species when breeding dogs.

In no species throughout the animal kingdom are there several hundred breeds or varieties unrecognisable from their original ancestors, as there are in the dog family. Each separate breed of dog is different from all the others in a variety of characteristics, and each breed is an artificial, man-made and man-devised product that has to conform to an intricate standard entirely its own. The Chihuahua, the Great Dane, and the Alsatian have few features in common, and yet it is necessary for the breeder to retain a number of special characteristics peculiar to his own chosen breed; and when he has done this and produced a specimen typical of this *created* breed it is essential, if it is to win prizes, that certain combinations of artificial features shall be present in the same individual—not such an easy matter as one might imagine, but it constitutes a problem that intrigues the dedicated breeder and creates the Fancy as well as the fancier.

And where does the brood bitch come in? She contributes a half of the inheritance and, in addition, she comes in as the reservoir of all the breed features and as the factory and the milk-bar that can turn out and deliver the goods. The sire is of great importance, too, as the force that can put the operation of breeding into motion and supply an equal share of the genes that will modify the development of fractions of each member of the litter, with a hope that the combinations and permutations of genes presented by the two parents may produce a perfect specimen of the breed.

Breeding is always something of a gamble. The odds against the breeder may be reduced by a knowledge of form, but there is no royal road to success. If there were, it would be the end of dog breeding.

Breeding precautions

No bitch should be bred from before she has finished growing, never before her second heat, and better at her third. Very few breeders will agree with the last statement, mainly because it does not fit in with the general economics of kennel management.

A good many bitches are kept intact until after this age so that they may be shown, and they are often bred from quite successfully, later even than the third season.

Prior to the time when she is expected to come into season the bitch needs regular exercise and suitable nourishment. She should remain lean and active rather than become fat and lethargic.

A bitch should be wormed a few weeks before she is due in season, and following this she should be isolated as far as possible to avoid reinfestation from worm eggs passed out in the droppings of other dogs or puppies. The dosing should be repeated between the 5th and 6th weeks following the mating. The choice of the anthelmintic is important. Any veterinary surgeon will supply a safe and effective vermicide that will not cause purging or bowel irritation. A few of the vermifuge medicines in common use may be too drastic for use during pregnancy.

Vaccination is a matter that needs consideration in the bitch of, let us say, two or three years of age, from whom it is intended to breed, because a bitch that has been immunised as a puppy may, in two or three years, have lost her immunity unless she has been the round of shows or mixed freely with other dogs outside the kennels.

This applies principally to those bitches that have received no booster injections since their original vaccination. In such, the re-vaccination or (at the least) a booster dose should be given at least a month before the expected time of mating.

Vaccination should not be carried out *after* mating, or certainly not before the 40th day of pregnancy. If for any reason it becomes absolutely necessary to vaccinate the bitch *after* the 40th day or at any time after this, and before the birth of her puppies, it is essential the puppies should be vaccinated with a modified live virus at the 9th week, and again at their 15th week, with a booster at six months. The reason is that when the bitch is vaccinated during pregnancy her milk will contain antibodies that may nullify any living vaccine that can safely be injected into them. The result may then well be that the puppies will be entirely dependent upon the original antibodies in the milk, and when these diminish and disappear from the puppies' systems they will be wide open to infection. This is why the second injection at fifteen weeks and the booster at six months become so imperative.

If leptospiral or virus hepatitis should appear in the kennel during the period of pregnancy, the bitch should be injected against these two diseases with a *killed* vaccine, not with a living one. The veterinary surgeon will, of course, be quite aware of this.

Radiography, in an attempt to determine the existence or otherwise of pregnancy, may be injurious both to the bitch and her puppies.

In any case, X-ray diagnosis of pregnancy is seldom of any great value, without special apparatus, before the 7th week of pregnancy, when it should not be required.

It is possible for skilled fingers (but, please, not the owners!) to diagnose pregnancy between the 22nd and 29th days. About the 22nd day in the smaller breeds, and the 24th day in the larger, the miniature embryos can be felt at the pelvic brim and further forward, below the backbone, as a 'string of beads'. A few days later, fluid will have formed around them, contained within the membranous sacs (allantois and amnion), and the beads will not be so easily felt.

Feeding the brood bitch

During the important month prior to mating, the prospective dam should receive an adequate *mixed diet*, containing meat, biscuit, some vegetable material, and up to 4 per cent fat. Workers at the University of Chicago found that bitches fed before and during pregnancy with this quantity of fat had a better reproductive record than those fed on exactly the same ration but minus the fat. Their puppies showed also a higher weight gain than those in other groups on test rations.

Vitamins must be added to the diet from a month before mating until the puppies are weaned, but some care is needed here.

When fats containing vitamin A are fed in amounts up to 4 per cent, they may have a neutralising effect upon vitamin E, which is regarded as the fertility vitamin, and it is advisable to continue the 4 per cent fat ration and to increase the vitamin E intake, giving up to 10 to 25 units a day, according to the size of the dog. If this happens to be slightly in excess of requirements it should do no harm. The vitamin E can be obtained, without prescription, as tablets of alpha-tocopheryl in the appropriate dosage.

Alternatively, extra vitamin E can be added to the food: egg yolk, beef liver, plus vegetable seed oils such as pure linseed oil, one to two teaspoonsful daily, in divided doses; or lightly cooked vegetables such as lettuce, cabbage or spinach can be included in the diet, when obtainable.

Many foods contain small quantities of vitamin E, but as it is so easily obtainable in tablet form it can be administered in this way when 'cooking time' is limited.

The *minimum* amount required for the bitch is 1·5 milligrams (mg) to each kilogram (about 2 lb) bodyweight. For a 30 lb bitch this would be approximately 25 mg or 30 units of vitamin E. Presuming that at least half the vitamin E is supplied in the daily diet, this would need an extra 15 units of alpha-tocopheryl in tablet form (10 units of Vitamin E=8·2 mg d-alpha-tocopheryl acid succinate). (*See also* chapters 11 and 12.)

Calcium and phosphorus are essential to the bitch both before and during pregnancy as well as after her parturition. She must build up a reserve in her liver and bone marrow over and above the amount needed during pregnancy, to maintain bone formation within the puppies in her womb. A further reserve will be needed to cope with her lactation problem, and if she is unable to transfer sufficient calcium from her blood to her milk she is likely to go down with milk fever (hypocalcaemia) either at the beginning or at the height of her lactation.

The calcium and phosphorus should reach the bitch in her food in, as nearly as possible, 1·2 parts calcium to 1 part phosphorus in order that the calcium may be absorbed into the bloodstream of the bitch. Nor must the calcium content of the bowel be too high or the excess will combine with some of the 4 per cent of fat to form an insoluble calcium soap, with resulting indigestion and constipation. The bitch will then go short of fat, and there is a danger that her puppies may lack sufficient calcium to form normal bone.

When given in the form of sterilised bone meal, this should contain 56 per cent of available calcium and about 40 per cent of available phosphorus, which approximates with the correct level. Too much bone meal may cause concretions within the rectum, and resulting constipation.

When the proportions of calcium and phosphorus are incorrect, the administration of vitamin D, either as calciferol or in the form of cod-liver oil, may be sufficient to overcome any ill effects. This is why cod-liver oil is regarded by breeders as the main safeguard against rickets. Another way to get calcium into the pregnant bitch is to give an extra ration of from 4 to 10 oz of fresh milk daily.

In general, her diet should contain variety in the type of protein fed to her. This can be done by alternating meat with mutton, or liver, and adding cooked vegetables, if she will take them. Broths made by boiling cabbage, carrots, leeks, and potatoes, with the addition of chopped-up meat, which is allowed to cool, and is fed once daily, solves the protein problem; and a little bone meal plus cod-liver oil gets over the calcium/phosphorus difficulty. Milk may be regarded as the desirable extra.

The changes may be rung with tripe, boiled sheep's heads, heart (not too frequently), melt in small quantities, and imported rabbit flesh. Sterilised bone meal may be added in the proportion of a half-teaspoonful to each quarter-pound of mixed food.

Ample supplies of both vitamin A and D are especially needed during the first five weeks of pregnancy, the time when the various anatomical features of the puppy's development are being sorted out. Both these vitamins are contained in cod-liver oil, and one teaspoonful daily is sufficient for small breeds, while the large breeds may take a tablespoonful.

The quantity of food given should be relatively greater during the last five weeks of pregnancy, and the protein should be increased until one-third of the whole ration consists of meat in some form.

Thirst increases, and may be satisfied by extra milk at this time. Exercise should be maintained in reasonable limits on level ground, if possible, up to within a few days of whelping, when it should be reduced to frequent short walks on the lead.

2

The Sexual Apparatus

A brief consideration of the sexual organs, especially those of the bitch, will explain the terms used in the next chapter and make the matter of fertility and conception easier to understand.

THE MALE ORGANS

The penis The penis of the dog is remarkable in that it contains a bone, the *os penis,* and has an erectile portion (glans) at either end, with the posterior portion much better developed than the anterior.

It may be regarded as having a middle portion supported by the os penis, a root (the posterior glans,) and a free extremity lying in front of the bony os penis. The undersurface of the body contains the *urethra,* the tube that gives passage to the urine, and within the penis the urethra lies in a channel, open below in the form, on section, of an inverted V.

It is this bony casing around the greater portion of the urethra that renders the dog prone to urethral obstruction caused by small, chalky masses (calculi) which are liable to become trapped near the posterior entrance into this bony canal.

The anterior glans is small as compared with that of most male mammals, other than the ruminants, but the posterior glans, rare except in the dog family, can enlarge during copulation to the size of a golf ball in a dog of one of the larger breeds. It then becomes gripped by the constrictor muscle lying just within the vulva of the bitch; this prevents withdrawal and produces what is termed 'a tie'. It thus acts as a cork in a bottle and prevents the escape of the semen secreted by the dog for from 10–20 minutes, or longer, while the tie lasts.

Although a 'tie' increases the chances of the semen travelling along the Fallopian tubes of the bitch to meet with the eggs (ova), a tie is not always essential, and many bitches after an imperfect service without a 'tie', do conceive in normal fashion, provided a certain amount of semen is passed into the vagina (genital passage) of the bitch.

The testicles These are two oval organs, slightly flattened on the medial surface; each contained in its own compartment of the sac (scrotum) in which they are lodged.

Their upper (dorsal) surfaces and their two extremities are connected with the *epididymis* and the *spermatic cord.*

The epididymis of each testicle consists of an elongated mass formed by the windings of a very long tube with a small lumen. The upper part of the epididymis is adherent to the testicle, while the tail end, containing the extremity of the coiled tube, passes down through the *inguinal canal*, a passage through the groin; together with blood vessels, muscle, and connective tissue, it forms the spermatic cord. The semen of the dog is secreted continuously throughout copulation and passed through the epididymis, down through the duct in the spermatic cord, and eventually passes through the urethra within the penis and emerges at the anterior end of the glans penis.

The semen of the dog is a watery fluid secreted in considerable quantity during copulation, and especially throughout the tie, during which it is rhymically 'pumped' through the urethra of the dog into the vagina of the bitch. A small dog, a Pomeranian for example, will deliver 5 to 10 cc of semen, or approximately 2 to 3 teaspoonsful, while a large dog may deliver 2 to 4 tablespoonsful.

One drop contains many thousands of actively swimming, very minute sperms. Under a high-power microscope they resemble tadpoles, with an oval body and long tail that moves about rapidly and propels the sperm through the fluid. Most of the fluid in the semen of the dog is secreted

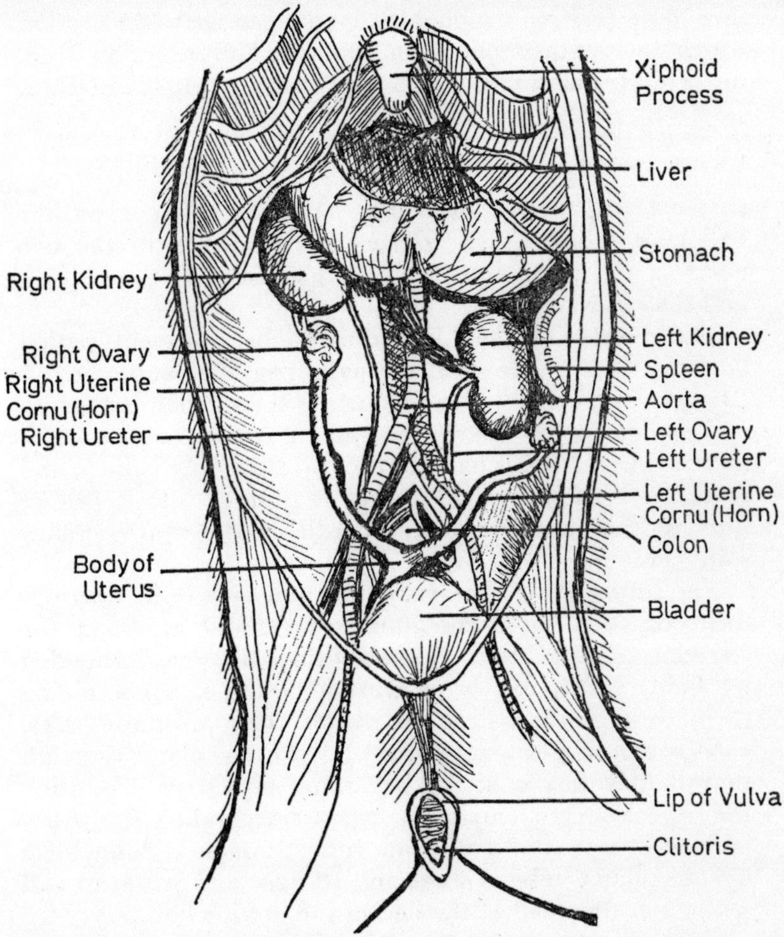

Figure 1 The female organs from below, intestines removed

by the prostate gland, which is somewhat like a walnut in size and shape in a dog of Cocker Spaniel size, and lies at the mouth (exit) of the bladder, giving passage to the urethra which passes through its substance. The secretion from the prostate gland passes through two ducts into the urethra.

THE FEMALE ORGANS

In the bitch, these consist (Fig. 1) of the two ovaries, the Fallopian tubes, which connect the ovaries with the two horns of the uterus, the vagina, the vestibule, the clitoris, and the external vulva.

The ovaries of the bitch during the quiescent period between 'heats' are rather small, pea-like, and each is partly surrounded by a sac known as the ovarian bursa.

The ovaries lie below the lumbar bones, and each is attached by a fibrous band to the corresponding kidney, and to the last rib. The right kidney is situated a little farther forward than the left, and accordingly the ovaries follow suit.

The substance of the ovary from the time of its development contains egg-production centres, and at about the start of the season (oestrus) some of these become surrounded by fluid, which causes protrusion of the sacs containing them, through the wall of the ovary. These protruding sacs, each containing an egg (ovum) burst on or about the 10th to 14th day following the beginning of oestrus, liberating the egg. The egg enters the bursa surrounding the ovary and travels to the Fallopian tube through a funnel-like opening. Each tube is short and straight and passes to and penetrates, the wall at the end of the uterine horn.

The egg meets the fast-swimming sperms within the Fallopian tube. The fertilised egg travels into the uterine horn and, after a while, becomes attached to the lining of the uterus (endometrium) where it develops its coverings (allantois and amnion), quickly becomes surrounded by fluid, and develops into the embryo and, eventually, into the fully formed puppy (foetus).

The uterus In the quiescent period the uterus of the maiden bitch is made up of two horns (cornua) of small size, joined to a short body in the shape of a Y. The horns extend nearly as far forward as the kidneys, and join the body of the uterus near the front rim of the pelvis at the level of the bladder.

Where they enter the body of the uterus there is a valve-like structure, closed by muscular tissue, known as the *cervix*. This projects slightly into the lumen of the uterine body with its other orifice within the vagina. Normally it is tightly closed, but during oestrus it opens a little to permit the sperms to pass through it. During whelping it dilates a great deal so that the vagina and the greatly enlarged uterine horns become continuous.

The vagina This is lengthy in the bitch and consists of a tube with a corrugated lining, its floor pierced at its lower end by an aperture leading into a short urethra which carries the urine from the bladder into the vagina at about the level of the pelvic brim. The corrugation allows for dilatation at whelping time.

The lower end of the vagina opens into a short tube which has a smooth lining known as the *vestibule*. The vestibule is surrounded by a circular constrictor muscle and contains two elongated masses of erectile tissue as well as the clitoris, which is a sense organ. During mating, the constrictor muscle contracts and the erectile tissue expands. This grips the penis of the dog behind the posterior glans and prevent its withdrawal for a matter of from 10 to 25 minutes. This is the explanation of the 'tie'.

The vulva This external opening of the genital canal takes the form of a vertical slit, the outer layer being hairless skin and the internal, mucous membrane. The upper angle (commisure) is blunt, and the lower free and pointed. The clitoris is lodged in a large fossa at the lower angle.

During oestrus the vulva enlarges. The ovaries increase in size owing to the development of a number of surface sacs (follicles) each containing follicular fluid and an egg (ovum). These rupture at short intervals, a somewhat variable time after the start of oestrus, usually between the 10th and 15th days, but the period may be less or greater in certain bitches.

The eggs have to meet and fuse with sperms within a limited time since the free life of the sperms is a very few days.

The uterus enlarges considerably during the period of pregnancy. While previously it was little greater in diameter than a goose-quill, even in comparatively large bitches, it expands during the nine weeks of pregnancy until each horn may be up to 10 inches in length and up to 3 inches in diameter in a moderate-sized bitch, and much larger in the heavier breeds. The pregnant horns fold upon themselves, forming a '2-storey uterus'.

The endometrium lining each horn of the womb carries alternating bands of mucous membrane and highly vascular zones. Each vascular zone is responsible for the nourishing of a single puppy.

3

Fertility and Infertility

The degree of fertility varies considerably in different kennels even when the standard of management is equally efficient. There is a possibility that fertility and infertility may to some extent be hereditary. It follows that when infertility is inherent, the strain must die out. There is little doubt that in many species that were common in the past, fertility has been too low to cope with the death rate, and so the species has now disappeared.

It is commonly accepted as a fact—and a provoking one—that a pedigree bitch that has been mated repeatedly to one or more stud dogs, known to be fertile, without achieving pregnancy, will frequently hold to the first mongrel dog with which she achieves a mésalliance.

Nevertheless, it takes two to produce a litter, and the establishment of pregnancy depends upon normal male sperms (spermatazoa) contacting a normal ovum in a suitable position in the Fallopian tube (between the ovary and the horn of the uterus) while the ovum is still receptive and the sperms are present in numbers, vigorous, and capable of secreting a hormone of their own that will act as a solvent and assist one or more of the sperms to penetrate the wall of the ovum.

The retention of vigour by the sperms and the ability of the ovum to receive and fuse with the body of a sperm can also be influenced by the condition of the Fallopian tube of the female and the degree of acidity or alkalinity of the fluid it contains, irrespective of the possibility of any infection of the tube itself by bacteria.

The time when eggs (ova) may be liberated from the ovary of the bitch varies not only with the breed, but also with the individual, and although one may believe that the optimum time for mating is somewhere between the 12th and 15th days after the beginning of heat, the real truth is that the right time is the period during which the bitch is actively seeking the male. In other words the precise moment can be decided only by the bitch herself and only when dog and bitch are free to mate at will.

The best manifestation of the right moments is still registered by the sideways cocking of the tail of the bitch when accosted by the male, or even when a hand is pressed lightly down on her loin.

In establishments where it is possible to permit mating at the will of the participants, it may be found that the bitch may seek service at any time from the 10th to the 21st day following the first sign of bleeding at the vulva, but it has been pointed out by experienced breeders that on occasions a bitch may prove receptive much earlier than this, even at the 5th day. It is equally certain that some, too, may ovulate much later than the accepted time, which may imply delayed ovulation, or a continuous shedding of ova over a somewhat protracted period.

We have a record of a Cocker bitch, mated at sundry intervals between the 12th and 16th days which actually became pregnant to a promiscuous mating with several dogs of dubious parentage, four weeks later. There are a number of similar happenings on record.

The most suitable time for mating can often be decided by the use of a microscope that enables the observer to determine the time when white cells first appear in a vaginal smear. Mating should be effected within 24 hours of their appearance. This examination can be carried out by a veterinary surgeon.

The obstacles to conception are numerous and include:

In the male

A stud dog may be overworked or may be used at a time when his efficiency index is low.

Rarely, a stud dog may be too fat from overfeeding and

lack of exercise, but this seldom applies to those used frequently.

Dogs, like bitches, are more active and more fertile at some times of the year than at others, although this fact is not generally recognised.

Male fertility is at its lowest between November and January, and it increases according to the number of hours of daylight between April and August.

Some dogs used at stud become over-excited and do not appear ever to acquire the necessary technique.

Fertility depends, also, largely upon diet, and it is increased during any season of the year by the addition of green vegetable material to the food, corresponding with the period when similar green material forms a considerable part of the stomach contents of the wild animals. It is this material that has always provided the main diet of the wild hunting dogs.

Some dogs, which serve normally, secrete quantities of semen entirely devoid of sperms. In other dogs, sperms may be present in their thousands, but provided with faulty heads, or they may be devoid of tails, or be in some other way defective. Faults such as these can be determined by a veterinary surgeon by microscopical examination of the semen.

In some bitches, the vaginal fluids may be capable of destroying the male sperms, particularly those from certain sires to which the tissues of the bitch may display an allergic reaction to semen.

The practice of washing out the vagina of a bitch with a mild alkaline solution is of doubtful value, although at one time it was regarded as useful.

In the female

The number of ova produced by a bitch and fertilised by male sperms is usually greatly in excess of the number of puppies finally born.

A great many of the embryos are absorbed during early

pregnancy, and when the number of ova fertilised is low no puppies may be born.

It is by no means unusual to take bitches to a veterinary surgeon for pregnancy diagnosis on or about the 23rd day following service. At this time the number of developing foetuses can actually be counted, feeling as they do at this time 'like a string of beads'. At about the 30th day the developing embryos become surrounded by fluid, when it is harder to diagnose pregnancy again until about the 5th to 6th week.

It is by no means unusual for these early embryos to be absorbed completely, to the great disappointment of the owner.

In one Boxer bitch, served by a Great Dane, eighteen puppies were present in a state of early development when the bitch was operated upon (ovohysterectomy) on the 21st day following service. It is very unlikely that more than a minor proportion of these would have persisted up to the date of whelping.

Under similar conditions, as many as twenty embryos have been found in process of development in a Cocker Spaniel, and there is a record of another bitch of this breed which at her first parturition actually delivered eighteen puppies, none of which survived.

The average bitch does not express all her eggs at one time but spreads the process over 1 to 4 days. These ova have to meet the sperms while they are both still viable. The sperms take only a short while (less than an hour probably) to travel from the cervix, along the uterus, and into the Fallopian tubes, where they will encounter the newly expressed ova, if the time of service is well chosen.

The life of the sperms is not normally lengthy. It is unlikely they will remain alive and active for more than 48 hours, and the period may be less than this, depending upon the nature of the fluids present in the Fallopian tubes. It is to be presumed that owing to a variety of circumstances the life of the sperms must vary a great deal according to the constitution and health of the donor.

In view of these statements it would seem that after the bitch has willingly accepted service, it should be repeated 48 hours later to ensure the best results. If the interval is greater than this, ova may be fertilised at lengthy intervals so that the last puppies born in the litter may be several days older—or younger—than some of the others, reckoning from the moment of conception, with the result that the period occupied in whelping may be lengthened, and some of the puppies may prove stronger, or weaker, than the others.

One kennel, in which bitches run continually with the prospective sire, is quite free from infertility problems but as the same bitch may be mated frequently at intervals of one of two days, whelping troubles are frequent and there is some apparent reduction in the number of puppies born alive, and in the vitality shown by a proportion of the living puppies.

As a general rule, the average number of puppies born in a litter remains fairly constant in individual breeds, with the tendency for large breeds to have large litters, and vice versa. It is possible that overcrowding in the small uterus of a small bitch may reduce the number of foetuses merely because of lack of room in which to develop. Male embryos have lower vitality than female, and the result may be a preponderance of females in small litters. Bitches up to three years produce the largest litters, after which the size of the litter lessens. The number of puppies in each litter frequently decreases considerably in advancing age but the proportion of males and females in the litter does not materially alter. The size of a litter decreases as the sire gets older, so that dogs over eight years of age tend to sire rather smaller litters. Bitches produce the largest litters during the first three years of life, and after this the numbers of puppies born becomes less, though the ratio of males and females is not affected. Generally, more males are born between October and December. In the larger breeds, as well as in the smaller, on an average throughout the year the proportion of males to females is from 106–125:100.

4

The Development of the Puppy

This subject needs only brief discussion. The fertilised ovum passes down the Fallopian tube and enters the cavity of the uterus. At this time, the lumen of the uterine horn is small and contains only a moderate quantity of fluid, which is secreted by the endometrium, the name given to the lining of the womb.

For some days the fertilised ovum lies in this fluid, absorbing some of it and being nourished by it, as well as being protected against temperature changes and desiccation.

The lining of the uterus of the bitch is not alike throughout but at intervals carries bands (zones) which contain additional blood vessels. The developing egg eventually becomes adherent to one of these zones. All the time its cells have been dividing and multiplying in an orderly manner so that at a very early age the tissues that are to grow within a few weeks into the natural and various organs of the body have their foundations devised and established.

Soon after this adhesion between the puppy and the womb has taken place, two separate sacs or water bags begin to envelop the puppy.

The one nearest the puppy is at first a rather close fit, resembling a small plastic bag. Its outer surface adheres to a small area of a zone upon the uterine wall, the sac gradually becoming larger; it contains a slippery, glutinous fluid. The sac is termed the *amnion*, and through its walls blood is filtered to nourish the young puppy, by a process known as *osmosis*. Very fine capillary blood vessels in the wall of the amnion come into close contact with others within the lining of the uterus. The term *osmosis* applies to the interchange of substances, mainly in solution, between adjoining capillaries. The capillaries are very fine, thinner even than hairs, and their walls are frequently only one cell thick.

If we took a jar of 2 per cent salt solution and another containing a 1 per cent solution, covered the tops with a very fine, non-waterproof membrane, then placed the jars end-to-end with their moist membranes in close apposition, we should find after a while that the fluids in the two jars were no longer 2 per cent and 1 per cent solutions but that water had passed from one jar, and salt from the other jar until the contents of each were of equal concentration.

Exactly the same thing happens when two thin-walled capillaries are in close apposition, containing blood of unequal concentration as regards the salts and protein substances they contain. Substances in stronger concentration pass into the other capillary, while fluid passes from that containing the weaker dilution into its neighbour.

This is how the puppy is fed in the uterus. There is no direct circulation between the mother and the foetus but food substances pass through the capillaries of the maternal placenta (a cushion of capillaries lining the uterus), into the foetal portion of the placenta, and from this into the puppy's bloodstream through the blood vessels which travel through the umbilical cord into the circulation of the puppy.

A second and larger sac, the allantois (Fig. 2), surrounds the greater part of the amnion, with a considerable space between them, the space becoming filled with a thin clear fluid.

The thick fluid in the amnion is destined to act as a lubricant when the puppy is in process of birth. It is known to breeders as the 'second water bag' because it bursts later than the first water bag, the allantois, which often protrudes through the vulva of the bitch for some time before the puppy appears.

The amniotic fluid contains a small amount of the excretion from the puppy's intestines and, occasionally, some semi-solid faeces. If the puppy has suffered from 'foetal diarrhoea' the contents may be dark green or yellow. The pigment present may represent that from bile secreted normally by the liver. Many breeders panic needlessly when discoloured fluid appears in the second water bag. The fluid also contains some blood serum, sebum (secretion from the skin follicles), and a little saliva.

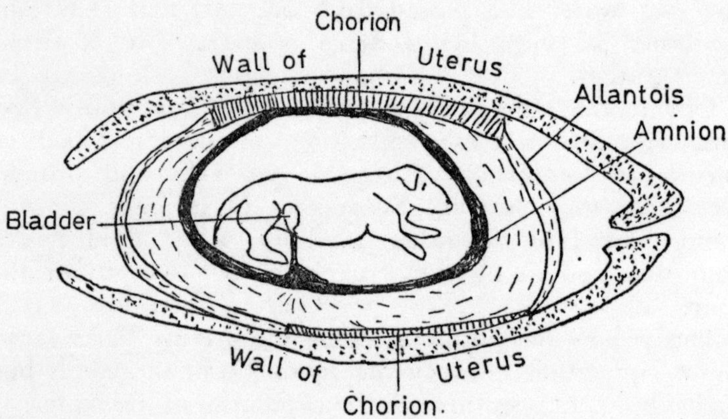

Figure 2 The layers of the womb. The highly vascular connection between the uterus and amnion is termed the 'chorion'

The larger amount of fluid contained in the second water bag, the allantois, is derived from the urine passed from the puppy's bladder through the urachus, into the allantoic cavity. The membranes and the fluids act as buffers protecting the growing puppy against external injury.

The uterus begins to enlarge, but seldom contains much fluid until the 4th week, after which it dilates rapidly, mainly to accommodate the large amount of urine passed from the kidneys of each puppy into the allantoic cavity.

During development the enlarged and elongated horns of the uterus fold upon themselves so as to form two layers of uterus, one superimposed upon the other.

Birth

The processes of birth are regulated mainly by the timely secretion of hormones from the pituitary gland (posterior portion) into the bloodstream of the bitch. This gives rise to uterine contractions intended to propel the puppies through the vagina and vulva.

As the fluid pressure within the uterus increases, and when the pituitary hormone secreted into the bloodstream sends the uterine muscles into a series of contractions, the allantoic sac of the first puppy to be born is pressed and squeezed against, and eventually protrudes through, the dilating cervix. Some puppies come head first (anterior presentation), others come tail first (posterior or breech presentation). When, in this position, the puppy lies on its back, the presentation is known as lumbo-pubic. Quite frequently the two positions alternate so that an anterior presentation is followed by a posterior and vice versa.

In young bitches the first puppy may take some hours to make its appearance. In older bitches that have borne litters, parturition is more rapid unless there is an obstruction.

The chief impediments are:

(*a*) a head that is wider than the pelvic girdle;
(*b*) a head turned back upon the shoulder or jammed beneath the pubic brim;
(*c*) an oversize puppy or one with an enlarged (dropsical) abdomen or a hydrocephalus (fluid in the skull);
(*d*) a posterior presentation, often with the head of the next puppy also in the vagina;
(*e*) doubling of the body of the puppy with the head and hindquarters retained;
(*f*) two puppies, side by side.

There are many other possible complications but these are the most common, and each needs professional assistance.

The afterbirth

Normally, the placenta and the two sacs (or their walls) form the so-called afterbirth (Fig. 3), and they should pass out, either attached to the umbilical cord (which passes through the puppy's navel), or follow the birth within a few minutes, with the help of further straining. If it appears to be easy to remove, the afterbirth may be pulled gently and steadily so long as it is freeing itself from the uterine wall. If one or more afterbirths (counted to see if they

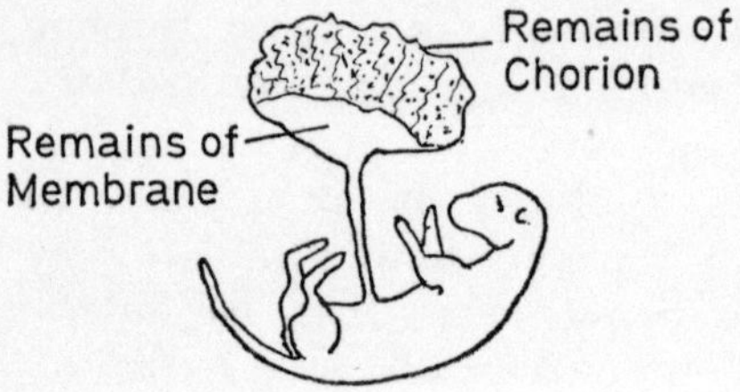

Figure 3 Puppy with afterbirth attached

correspond with the number of puppies born) appear to have been left behind, a veterinary surgeon will give a hormone injection to effect their passage. The retention of one or more afterbirths may set up metritis and even cause death.

Many bitches endeavour to swallow their afterbirths. Although some breeders assert they do not vomit them, many bitches actually do so, and quite often a bitch may be 'off her feed' for a day or two after devouring them. At one time it was believed that eating the afterbirth caused the milk of the bitch to flow more freely.

The milk often seems to be absent at the time of birth but if the puppies are strong and active the milk usually appears and suffices for the puppies so long as one is able to squeeze one or two drops from each teat. Milk is secreted as the puppy sucks. The bitch must receive plenty of fluid at this stage, and warm, sweetened milk and beef broth are good.

Bitches should be disturbed as little as possible. Care is needed occasionally for the first few days to ensure that *all* the puppies get their turn at the milk-bar and to see that the bitch does not turn sides and lie on one or more of them. This applies mainly to the larger breeds.

5

Saving the Newborn

The puppy may be born completely wrapped, head and all, in the unbroken amnion, though more often, especially in prolonged or difficult births, the membrane will rupture and liberate the lubricating content.

Nevertheless, in quite a number of puppies, born alive, there may be inability to begin breathing, owing to suffocation by the presence of a particularly thick membrane; or it may be that a young mother does not at first realise that she has to tear away this wrapping. When bitches are left unattended during whelping, more healthy puppies are, probably, lost in this way than by any other means.

It is also very important to determine whether all the puppies have come away or if one is retained, or even more. Labour pains may cease after a certain number have been delivered. Palpating the abdomen may help in making a decision, but after a prolonged labour the uterus will go into a state of firm contraction and may be mistaken for a puppy. Quite a lot of bitches suffer from uterine inertia. Either they get no pains, or pains that are ineffectual, or after passing one or two puppies the pains ceasc. A veterinary surgeon should then be called.

As soon as the covering membranes have been removed either by the bitch or the attendant, it is necessary to decide whether or not the puppy is breathing. Quite commonly the moment it takes air into its lungs it cries. This is a good sign if it happens immediately after birth and if, at the same time, the puppy makes vigorous movements when the bitch licks it. Such a puppy is best left alone and re-examined half an hour later to make certain it has attached itself to a teat.

During the process of whelping, a bitch often becomes

anxious and restless, and inclined to move from corner to corner of her bed. Unless closely watched she may easily deposit herself, usually stern-first, upon a healthy puppy, recently born, and squash or smother it. To guard against this a hint from the pig breeders who experience a similar problem is worth knowing.

The easiest way to turn a big, box-type bed into a much safer whelping box is to bore holes in opposite sides of the box and push lengths of broomstick through them, as shown in Fig. 4.

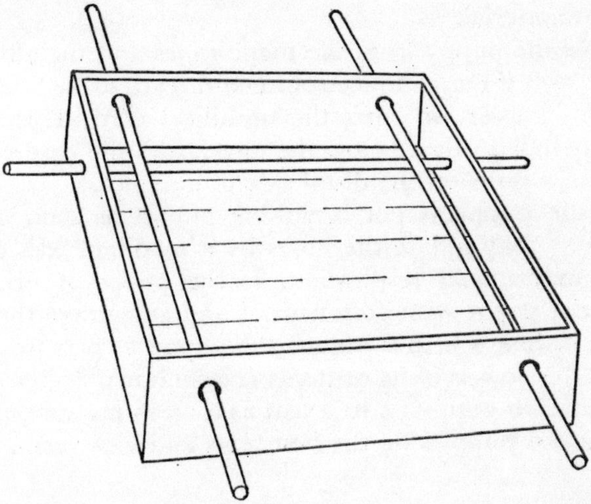

Figure 4 Design for whelping box

Two such lengths should be sufficient, but a third may be inserted at right angles to the others at the hinder end of the box.

Puppies can crawl beneath these protecting bars and are less likely to be crushed by the bitch, especially as she will have to settle down less forcibly in order to avoid the bars.

The best bedding during and immediately after whelping is sheets of newspaper, several layers of them. These may be replaced by fresh sheets when they become soiled.

Moreover, on paper, puppies do not become isolated or mislaid, as they may do when blanket material is used.

The main items to be attended to in readiness for whelping, are:

(*a*) Provide a source of heat, preferably an infra-red lamp suspended well above the puppies and centred upon one end or side of the box so that the occupants can select the degree of warmth they prefer. If hot-water bottles are used, always remember that the skins of both the bitch and her puppies will blister from far less heat than the human skin. So, make sure the hot-water bottles are well packed in blanket material.

(*b*) Free the puppy from the membranes and the afterbirth as soon as it is born. A piece of linen thread, soaked in iodine solution, is best for tying the umbilical cord. This should be done half an inch below the navel, and the cord divided by clean scissors on the distal side of the knot.

(*c*) If the puppy is not breathing almost as soon as it is born, one may inflate the lungs by a modified 'kiss of life', or begin artificial respiration. If the puppy is breathing regularly, dry it with cotton wool and encourage the bitch to lick it. She will thus induce the puppy to pass urine and empty the bowels of its contents (meconium).

(*d*) Get each puppy on to a teat as soon as possible, placing the weakest puppies on the best teats and vice versa.

Artificial respiration

The cubic capacity of a puppy's chest is quite small, and too heroic efforts to fill it may cause serious trouble. The lungs of the average human being are too strong to permit safe 'mouth-to-mouth' inflation of the lungs of a puppy. It is safer to employ a small-bore tube provided with a small hole in the lumen which may be covered and uncovered by the finger, with a close watch upon the amount of expansion induced. One must blow gently and at intervals of 2 to 3 seconds, allowing the puppy's chest to deflate as well as inflate in the correct rhythm.

A simple blow tube may be devised by removing the ink tube, the plastic cap, and the metal tip, from an ordinary ball-point pen (Fig. 5). The tapered end of the tube is inserted into the puppy's mouth, and respiration is started by blowing gently through the other end. If a small hole has been made half-way down the tube into the lumen of the air passage, this may be covered and uncovered at 2 second intervals with the tip of the finger. When the ribs

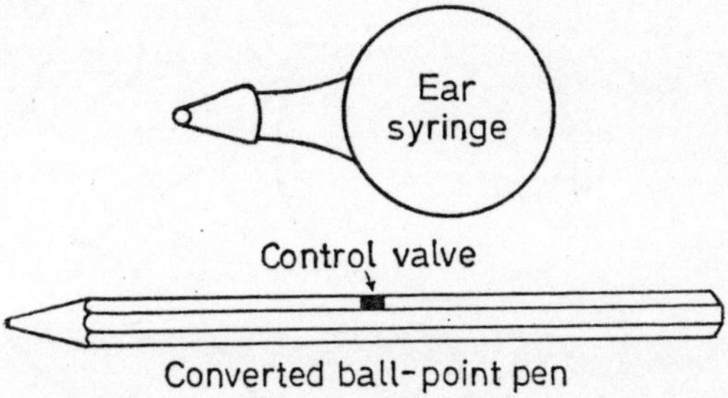

Figure 5 Simple aids to artificial respiration

rise as the lungs fill, stop blowing, and wait for the chest to empty by its own elasticity.

The hole bored into the lumen of the tube acts as a safety valve against the application of too much air pressure, and it can be closed with the tip of the finger if the pressure needs increasing. The inflation is continued until respiration is completely established. When the puppy of its own volition has taken one or more gulps of air artificial respiration may be carried on by the method shown in Fig. 6.

Whenever the puppy makes an effort to breathe but needs help, this is usually the better course to adopt and, in most instances, it is successful.

To carry out the operation, the puppy is held with the thumbs and fingers of both hands, its belly facing the operator and its back turned away.

Figure 6 Artificial respiration, showing direction in which puppy is turned by thumb and fingers

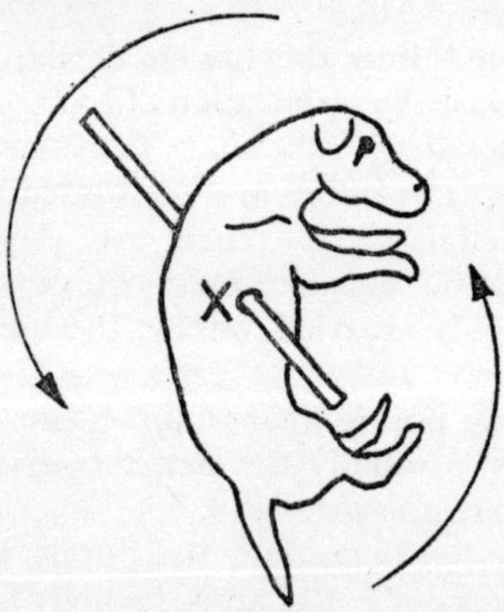

Figure 7 The cardboard model showing how the puppy is rotated

Imagine that the spot marked with an X in Fig. 7 is the spindle on or around which the puppy revolves in a clockwise direction.

First, the head turns backwards and downwards, the hind feet simultaneously rising upwards.

After this, the hind feet turn the circle and the head comes up again.

Each full turn of the puppy should take about 3 seconds, then after a second's rest the turning is repeated until normal breathing is restored.

It is good practice to draw the outline of a puppy on a piece of cardboard, cut it out with scissors, and transfix it on a skewer through the spot marked X. Revolve the puppy head down, tail up and so on, and become accustomed to the positions. Then try to imitate these without the skewer. This procedure is well worth learning as it saves more puppies than any other method when there is difficulty in getting them to start breathing.

Other instruments useful for inflating the lungs include a rubber ear syringe, which may be bought from a chemist; a small round plastic funnel which will fit snugly over the puppy's head. This has the advantage that when air is blown into the funnel, it travels down the puppy's nostrils rather than directly down the trachea. In the larger breeds the cardboard central tube of a toilet roll may be placed over the head or muzzle and blown through.

The ear syringe may also be used as a feeding bottle. The puppy is forced to suck against a vacuum within the bulb of the syringe and there is no fear of choking (provided an impatient attendant does not squeeze the rubber bulb!).

The syringe can be sterilised by boiling.

6

Puppy Mortality

The incidence of puppy mortality within the average breeding kennel between birth and six months old is not infrequently a third of the total number born. Even in kennels managed by careful and experienced breeders, a certain number of losses are not uncommon. This high rate of mortality does not involve only those litters that require professional attention. The rate is far higher among litters that fail to receive attention when it might be most helpful.

The fact that some of the most happy-go-lucky breeders may rear more than two-thirds of their puppies, and that badly cared-for mongrel bitches may rear up to 100 per cent, if permitted, proves nothing, apart from drawing attention to the fact that there are many possible factors involved; that many may never make their appearance in a particular kennel; and that when they do so, some may produce conditions apparently beyond the power of the owner to control.

To make the subject more easy to understand, we can divide it into:

(*a*) those dead at birth; (*b*) those in which death occurs within the first few days following apparently normal birth. This may involve a single puppy or a considerable part of the litter; (*c*) between weaning and six months of age; (*d*) between six and twelve months.

DEAD AT BIRTH

This may involve one or two puppies, or the complete litter. Generally speaking, the nearer the puppy is to the exit, the greater is its chance of survival, if there is nothing to retard delivery. Nevertheless, this first puppy to be born is the one least likely to survive if it is badly out of position, and especially if surgical interference is needed to effect delivery. The greatest risk, however, to the first-born results from undue panic on the part of the attendant.

If, instead of making frantic efforts at midnight to effect the delivery of a living, normal puppy before the cervix, vagina, and uterus have reached the state of readiness, the owner were to go to bed and sleep soundly until morning, he or she would probably find on awakening that the first puppy presented, as well as others, would be comfortably sucking.

In any case, a few hours' delay in the case of the untouched and uninfected vagina will not impede the efforts of the veterinary surgeon, if his services are finally required.

The exception is when the puppy is dead, swollen and partly decomposed—a very unlikely state of affairs—or when it is lying in such a position that it entirely precludes the possibility of normal birth. Even then, waiting a short while entails very little extra risk, provided no outside infection has been introduced by unclean fingers.

The retention of normal puppies for a few hours, within a healthy uterus, does little harm, since they are receiving oxygen and nourishment through the placenta, and have not yet inflated their lungs. Undue hurry is far more likely to be dangerous.

Now let us consider why one or more puppies should arrive dead among an otherwise strong and healthy litter. Firstly, take into consideration the size of the dead puppy. Is it a large, well-developed specimen, as usually is the case, or is it a small one, thin, shrivelled, and almost mummified?

During the early days of pregnancy it is usual for more eggs to be fertilised and implanted in the lining of the uterus preparatory to development and growth than finally survive. The defunct embryos undergo a process of resorption. As there may be insufficient time for this to be completed, the puppy is eventually delivered as a small specimen, not actually decomposed but apt to give this impression on account of its partial mummification. Sometimes it will be embedded in, or surrounded in its membranes, in company with a yellowish excrement which indicates that during its brief life in the uterus, the puppy suffered from 'foetal diarrhoea'.

When several puppies, or even the whole litter, are involved in this way, the underlying cause may have been either lack of vitamin A in the diet of the bitch at the early critical stage of embryonic development; or, alternatively, inability on the part of the bitch to make use of the vitamin A available. One reason for this may be the administration of wheat-germ oil, or vitamin E (the so-called 'fertility hormone') in excessive dosage. Too much vitamin E is capable of rendering the bitch unable to absorb the essential vitamin A. On the other hand, the lack of development may have been due to infection, possibly by *E. coli*.

There may be a variety of other causes of the death of a large, well-developed puppy prior to birth. The matter of sex may play a part since a large male has far less chance of survival during a somewhat prolonged parturition (in which uterine inertia may be involved) than a smaller female.

The other common cause is obstruction to the circulation of blood, involving an insufficient circulation of oxygen within the puppy's bloodstream. This often results from entanglement of the umbilical cord (carrying the blood vessels) around some part of the puppy's own body, or by its becoming imprisoned by the limbs of another puppy. Sometimes a rotation of the body of a puppy carries the cord, which is fairly long, around the abdomen, thereby diminishing or cutting off the circulation.

Another cause is that, frequently, puppies arrive in 'posterior presentation', in other words, 'tail first'. This may apply to alternate puppies but sometimes all, or almost all, arrive in this way.

The passage of the puppy is impeded, and the bitch makes strenuous 'forcing' efforts to keep it moving. Fluids are then squeezed down the nostrils and open mouth of the puppy and pass into the lungs. The result is that when the puppy eventually makes an effort to breathe it fails because the lungs are full of fluid; or in other words, the puppy is drowned.

A complete litter 'dead at birth', from a bitch that has been watched and not neglected, and has delivered her puppies without undue effort, is often the result of infection, frequently by a virus (distemper or hepatitis possibly) or sometimes by leptospira (rodent infection?) and even by common bacteria such as *E. coli*, a normal inhabitant of the intestine which, in certain circumstances, may become highly virulent.

The infection may result in death of the puppies and premature birth, or they may be retained until full term and delivered dead.

In some virus infections the puppies may be born dead without any visible signs of infection in the dam.

EARLY CARE

Whatever the age of the puppy, its prospect of surviving and growing up into a normal, healthy adult will be influenced largely by the type of owner into whose care it is delivered.

Although there can be no excuse for the guardian who 'couldn't care less', there is no doubt whatever that as many young puppies die (or become stunted in their development) as the result of undue fussing and unwarranted interference as from deliberate neglect.

While a certain amount of supervision is advisable, the nursing bitch should be disturbed as little as possible. Once in charge of a family, a bitch—whatever her position in the home may have been—undergoes a change of heart, and her immediate concern is now with her offspring rather than with humanity. Persistent interruption in the normal course of her maternal duties is apt to confuse her and upset her normal curriculum.

The birth will have, however, certain basic requirements that she will be unable to supply in a state of domestication.

These include a suitable and *private* environment, warmth, and food.

Bitches, in the house, prefer to choose their own sites for whelping and, so far as may be practicable, they should be humoured in this respect. Away from the family is preferable, and the settee in the drawing room should never be considered ideal, even for a Chihuahua.

The ideal whelping box has been described already, but as it is not always available in emergency it is essential to provide a flat surface and suitable bedding.

The latter may consist of a blanket folded over and over to make a soft bed that will fit into a convenient corner of a room not in general use. The blanket should be covered by a number of layers of newspaper—easily changed when required. Some kind of border should be devised to prevent puppies wandering away from the nest. Straw, haw, wood-wool and the like, may entangle the puppies or enable them to disappear from view. In addition such materials may harbour parasites, or may accidentally introduce infection.

A puppy needs a smooth, flat surface, to permit it to gyrate around its own posterior, an exercise that invariably brings its receiving end into contact with the teats of its mother.

Warmth is essential if puppies are to survive, and suck and sleep alternately. A whelping room, winter or summer, should be kept at a temperature of 70 to 75 degrees Fahrenheit. An infra-red lamp suspended over the bed at a height of never *less* than 24 or 30 inches, according to the type of lamp, is an advantage, and it is also advisable to hang it over one corner of the bed nearest the wall, so that the mother and family can get under or away from it, as they wish.

Skin scorching in mother and puppies can occur far more readily than in human beings. Hot-water bottles, even when well wrapped, can produce serious skin injuries, which do not make themselves evident (by skin sloughing) until several days following the injury.

If a bitch is to raise puppies to the best advantage, her diet before and after whelping is of the greatest importance.

After the puppies have arrived, one of the first requirements of the mother is fluid, and this goes hand in hand with protein requirements and additional fat.

Cows' milk (preferably whole and raw) provides most of these requirements, but to the town dweller, dried whole cows' milk, diluted with whatever form of processed milk obtainable, is a good substitute.

A small quantity of cod-liver oil (up to one tablespoonful a day for a medium-sized bitch) is a useful accessory.

After the first 48 hours, stews made from meat and bones (taking out the bones before offering it), plus a couple of eggs a day, given raw and beaten up, should reinforce the milk diet.

Raw bone marrow, if obtainable, may take the place of at least one of the eggs, but as it is a rich food, a good tablespoonful daily may be enough.

The number of puppies to be suckled needs consideration at times but as a general rule the safe number equals the total number of functioning teats, minus two.

Whether it is a good policy to attempt to preserve weak puppies is a matter for every owner to decide, but as it takes every available puppy (available meaning saleable) to make ends meet, the temptation to preserve the weak is strong.

A puppy that is being frequently nosed away from the bitch may be hand fed in the way previously described, beginning with a 20 per cent solution of glucose in warm water and then using warm whole milk diluted with a good brand of beef essence. The puppy should be held on a teat to obtain some of the mother's milk at alternate intervals, unless it has diarrhoea, when it is best taken off the bitch altogether and fed by hand.

When puppies appear weak and disinclined to suck, particularly if they make a continuous squealing noise reminiscent of seagulls overhead, it is high time to take them to the veterinary surgeon for penicillin injections, and subcutaneous glucose-saline. These symptoms often herald 'fading sickness', the scourge of so many kennels.

When litters arrive, obviously too large for the bitch to manage alone, a foster mother may be a godsend, but usually equally hard to procure.

A cat makes a good foster for one or two puppies but is seldom available just when required.

It is not wise, however, to destroy puppies unless obviously mis-marked or in some way defective, since litters have a knack of reducing their numbers when these are large; and hand-feeding on the lines discussed later in this chapter may retain substitutes against the time when members of the original team drop out.

From the viewpoint of safety, docking and the removal of dewclaws are best carried out between the 3rd and 5th days after birth. By this time the puppies will have full stomachs and are less given to bleeding than when they are older, if suitable precautions are taken.

Incidentally for those compelled by circumstance to carry out these operations at home, a reliable styptic (blood stopper) is powdered permanganate of potash crystals, applied on a pledget of damp cotton wool. I give this information because so many amateur breeders, unable to take their puppies to a veterinary surgeon, not infrequently lose their whole litters from inability to control bleeding after docking.

Many veterinary surgeons dock by a V-shaped incision, and insert one or two stitches. This prevents bleeding and ensures a good-looking tail stump. Nowadays, elastic ligatures are sometimes employed but they are not advisable since they cause pain and introduce infection. This statement will be almost furiously refuted by many breeders who dock their own puppies. In the writer's opinion the use, even in two-day-olds, of a local anaesthetic, surgical amputation and suturing, is still the most humane and the safest method of procedure.

During the first 12 weeks the remaining procedures most closely concerned with survival include worming, and vaccination against the three 'killer' diseases; distemper, hepatitis and leptospiral jaundice.

Unless (and sometimes 'when') the bitch has been thoroughly de-wormed before mating and again at some suitable stage of her parturition, most of her puppies will harbour round worms (ascarids) and whether they do the puppy any great harm, or not, will depend largely upon the food supply and the number of worms present. Quite often the main danger to puppies suffering from round worms is over-treatment prescribed by their owners.

Veterinary surgeons nowadays possess remedies that are completely effective against both round worms and tape-worms, but cause neither pain nor purging. It is far safer to take a specimen of the worms voided to the 'vet', and get him to supply the essential medicine with instructions as to its use.

Summarising the matter of breeding puppies, it is well to remember that the time to make the start is before they are conceived. Both the sire and dam require careful study both as regards pedigree and soundness to make certain, as far as one may be able, that neither exhibits or carries hereditary faults that may result in the loss of a portion or the whole of a litter, or the production of semi-cripples. Nor must one knowingly increase the number of carriers even if one obtains one good specimen out of the litter.

Never deceive yourself into thinking that even the most experienced breeder can decide at a glance whether a dog is both physically and genetically desirable. Genetic possibilities are not apparent in most cases and only the progeny can prove which are handed down.

This is where breeding becomes, and must always remain, a gamble. The only remedy—a partial one, perhaps—is always to keep a watchful eye on litters, whether of your own or other breeding, and upon the extended pedigrees that proclaim (or should proclaim) the litter's ancestry.

The laws of libel do not permit you to publish a list of desirable or undesirable sires or dams, but they do not prevent you forming your own conclusions.

Do not breed from stock too young or too old.

The second season, or even the third, is early enough in the case of a bitch. She cannot be expected to produce strong, healthy, fully developed puppies until she, herself, has completed the final stages of growth.

Never be in too great a hurry to see her mated. Although it is true that certain bitches ovulate on the 5th day of their season rather than on the 12th to 14th, in most instances more is lost through mating too early than too late.

It is waste of the dog's energy and time to mate a pair on two successive days, but mating at what is presumed to be the optimum moment, and then again either 48 or 72 hours later, is the most likely way to produce a litter.

Do not imagine that this second mating will be too late. Bitches vary enormously in their period of reception, and each needs individual study.

Many so-called infertile bitches remain so because they are mated at the wrong time, and it is often among these that the early starters may be found.

Conversely, there is on record the case of a golden Cocker bitch of uncertain age that used to mate at the normal time without ever conceiving, but showed continued swelling of the vulva for some weeks later. After four matings she was separated from the male but by accident she got out and was mated with him 28 days later. She conceived to this service and gave birth to nine puppies. A very similar record involves an exhibition Greyhound bitch.

Apparently, ovulation is not always synchronous with the cessation of uterine bleeding as so many breeders believe it to be.

Before mating, the bitch should be freed from worms or other parasites, internal and external. This includes fleas and lice.

Worming, preferably with a safe ascaricide supplied by a veterinary surgeon, can be repeated between the 5th and 6th weeks of pregnancy.

Correct feeding is especially needed during the first

month of pregnancy, the period during which the foundations of the puppy and the future adult are being laid down.

This is the time when a properly graduated scale of vitamins and minerals is essential. The appetite changes and becomes capricious. Scientists do not all agree that a bitch or any other animal can select the kind of food its body requires, but as many of our present ideas regarding animal behaviour may be superseded within the next few years it is wise not to be persuaded too readily.

Bitches, like other females early in pregnancy, develop likings for peculiar kinds of diet. Female carnivora in a state of nature eat the dry dung of herbivorous animals and, particularly, the contents of the paunch or stomachs of any animal they or their companions may kill.

Domesticated bitches at this period occasionally devour their own excrement or all manner of materials characterised as 'filth'. This is because they are (unknowingly) in search of vitamins and enzymes their bodies need for the development of the embryo puppies within their wombs.

We can help by ensuring a supply of vitamins A, B, D and E, and less commonly C. Vitamins A and D are present in cod-liver oil and in halibut oil. Vitamin E is present in wheat-germ oil or can be bought in tablet form as d-Alpha Tocopheryl. Vitamin B is present in yeast—ordinary cooking yeast—or in any of the yeast tablets on the market in profusion. (*See* Chapter 13.)

The actual quantities required are small, and overdosing with extra vitamins may be as bad as deficiency. One must guard, at this time, also against mineral deficiencies.

When it can be obtained, a little fresh rumen content from a freshly killed bullock, in the abattoir, is a very good addition to the diet; or this, too, may be obtained in a synthetic form.

To those who hold up their hands in horror at this unhygienic suggestion I would merely say that the dog is still fundamentally a wild animal and still needs its natural food. Paunch is far less harmful than many of the concoctions fed to dogs under high-falutin' names and is no more revolting than some of the dishes adored by the human epicure!

Even in our British summertime it is wise to be prepared as regards the provision of extra heating if it happens to be required. Infra-red heating is the safest and most convenient source provided it is kept sufficiently far above the bed and always a little to one side—never centrally—so that mother and puppies can choose the spot, and the temperature, which best suits them.

At the time of parturition the assistance provided by an experienced breeder will be all-sufficient so long as the course of labour is normal. When it is not, seek professional advice and turn a deaf ear to all well-meant advice from elsewhere.

And, in advance, keep one eye open for a possible foster mother in case of emergency.

DEATH OF PUPPIES WITHIN A FEW DAYS OF BIRTH

Death from pneumonia is a frequent sequel to the forced feeding of recently born puppies that have refused to suck or have been unable to do so for any reason. Puppies with cleft palate usually die from this condition. It is more common in short-faced varieties such as Pekingese, in which milk may return through the nostrils, and be inhaled.

Puppies fed with a teat or a dropper, or even with a teaspoon, often die in the same way, because the attendant is in too much of a hurry.

The safest way to feed a young puppy is to place about three drops of milk in a teaspoon; tilt the spoon until the milk rests in the tip of the spoon and, without pouring the milk, tip the spoon until the extremity rests between the puppy's lips. If it is hungry it will suck the milk from the spoon.

Even successful feeding may cause death if unsuitable mixtures are used. Pending the advent of a foster mother, young puppies kept warm by an infra-red lamp or a very well-covered hot-water bottle can be sustained for the first 24 hours by the subcutaneous injection of small quantities of glucose saline at 8 hourly intervals. This will have to be carried out by a veterinary surgeon. It eliminates death from pneumonia due to inhalation and prevents dehydration, which is one of the lethal factors associated with lack of fluid intake.

Occasionally, the bitch appears to take a dislike to a particular puppy, persistently noses it aside, and eventually pushes it out of the nest (*see* 'Fading Puppies', below). It seems that this behaviour is stimulated by something abnormal in the puppy's odour, and the habit is shared by a number of other animals even by seals which, living mainly in water, should not be so greatly affected by smell, it would seem. Frequently, such puppies harbour a bowel infection, and the mother probably realises the fact during cleaning operations.

Puppies of this type, removed from the dam, kept warm, given glucose saline injections plus a suitable antibiotic, frequently recover and may sometimes be taken back by the dam.

Losses of young puppies from haemorrhage following docking, crudely carried out by inexperienced operators, are far greater than would be believed. This is particularly the case with Dobermanns and other breeds that require the short dock. Losses of the whole litter or a considerable part of a litter have been reported frequently. This operation should be performed by a veterinary surgeon.

FADING PUPPIES

This is a term relating to the loss of puppies during the first few days following birth. Such deaths may arise from a variety of causes but the term refers particularly to those that show a characteristic set of symptoms arising from an infection, although the organisms that cause the losses may be varied.

Puppies destined to die off in this manner are usually born easily, and feed and look quite well for the first one or two days, although in affected litters one or more may be born dead, but this is not to be regarded as usual. Usually, on the second day or possibly the third, one or more of the litter will cease to suck or suck for a few seconds and then let go. Very soon they begin to set up an almost continuous wailing cry reminiscent of the sounds made by seagulls circling overhead in need of food.

Nearly all affected puppies die, though one or more members of the litter will sometimes escape the disease and continue to suck and thrive normally.

The affected puppies feel cold and may give off a rather 'vinegary' odour. This seems apparent to the bitch who may push them away with her nose to the outer boundaries of the nest and, not infrequently, she may toss them out of the nest altogether. This type of illness appears to be caused by a number of different organisms although in most instances one organism is mainly responsible.

Nearly fifty years ago, when the writer first drew attention to the disease, the cause appeared to be a haemolytic streptococcus but in later years *E. coli*, staphylococci and, more recently, the hepatitis virus have been blamed. Before the advent of antibiotics, no useful treatment was known and whole kennels used to be wiped out by this disease. When penicillin came into use it was found to be almost specific but this was in the haemolytic streptococcus period and since then penicillin has not always proved successful. Taking the puppies off the bitch and keeping them warm, with subcutaneous injection of glucose salines saves some of the affected puppies, and in other litters subcutaneous injection of *E. coli* serum with or without penicillin may help.

The injection of the two latter immediately after birth throughout the whole litter and well before symptoms are shown, appears to be a routine measure well worth while in kennels where the condition has previously appeared.

Another causal factor, in some cases, is an allergic reaction on the part of the puppy to its mother's milk, and in some kennels where bitches have lost their puppies, it has been found that litters may often be reared if the puppies are taken off the dam before they suck, and placed with a foster mother.

It has been recorded by several breeders that bitch puppies surviving from affected litters often give birth to puppies which develop the disease, in their turn, and die, and in this way a strain may be wiped out.

7

Efficient and Inefficient Vaccination

As things are in the dog world at present, the efficient vaccination of puppies against distemper, hardpad, viral hepatitis and leptospiral jaundice is essential.

If only vaccination were compulsory, distemper could be practically eliminated from this country in a very few years. Other hosts are the ferret and weasel family, and, in all probability, foxes and wild dogs, where they exist.

Without vaccination the prospect of being able to rear any puppy to adult age is becoming more and more unlikely. There is no very effective treatment for distemper since it is a virus disease attacking the body and brain cells, against which modern antibiotics have no useful effect, other perhaps than helping to ward off certain secondary infections.

It is true that even the most efficiently carried out vaccination cannot be given a 100 per cent guarantee but the small percentage of failures compares favourably with those obtained by other forms of vaccination, both in animals and man.

To resist distemper successfully the puppy, after vaccination, must be able to produce antibodies capable of rendering inert the material introduced into the body in the course of outside (field) infection. A small percentage fail to do so. Whether the failure results from a genetic cause is uncertain. A strain that is unable to put up a resistance, normal or acquired, against so virulent a disease has little chance either of surviving or propagating its species. Many of the so-called failures do not arise from inability to acquire immunity after injection of vaccine but from technical errors in administration, which can be avoided. Among these are:

(*a*) A puppy may already be in the incubation stage of the disease when presented for vaccination, without any obvious symptom of the disease. Alternatively, it may be taken to a premises, or through an area, where the infection is present, for the purpose of vaccination.

(*b*) The colostrum, the first milk of a bitch, immune to distemper, may contain a variable content of antibodies derived from the mother, and the antibodies may remain present in the milk for days or weeks. Colostrum containing antibodies much resembles, in its effects, blood serum from a dog recently recovered from the disease. The effect of giving immune serum to young puppies may produce some temporary immunity of comparatively short duration, but during its presence this immunity may easily render inactive any vaccine injected with the intention of establishing a more permanent immunity.

The possible presence of antibodies in the milk of the bitch makes it inadvisable to inject vaccine at too early an age and 8 weeks is regarded as the most suitable age. There is, however, a possibility that even at this time the milk may contain some antibodies and it is, therefore, advisable to give a second injection of vaccine between the 12th and 14th weeks, keeping the puppy isolated for a further month following the second injection.

When a firm immunity is likely to have been established it is best to take the puppy out and about, where it will meet other dogs and people. Every challenge by distemper virus by other dogs that is successfully overcome following vaccination strengthens the immunity and acts as a booster.

Nevertheless, a booster should be given at the end of the first and second years of life, and again after another two years.

Not infrequently, quite old dogs go down with distemper even when they have been vaccinated as puppies, simply because in close domestication they may not for years come up against infection. Their immunity wanes, and when they are finally challenged they have lost much of their resistance.

(*c*) A 'booster' has not been administered at the time that immunity may have waned. If the dog has lived in an area where it encounters other dogs or if it has been regularly exhibited, and if it has been efficiently vaccinated at an early age, it should withstand challenge and remain free from distemper.

(*d*) The vaccine may have come from an unfortunate batch, but this is a very rare occurrence. Veterinary surgeons are particularly careful never to use an outdated sample or to leave vaccine for any length of time out of a refrigerator. One can imagine possible delays in transit when parcels might be exposed to warm temperatures, but this must be a very unlikely reason for failure.

(*e*) In spite of the vendor's assurance, the puppy may never have been vaccinated. Certificates of vaccination are usually given by veterinary surgeons, and when buying a puppy it should be asked for.

There are still a few fanciers who maintain that they do not believe in vaccination, or have some infallible means of side-stepping infection. Few of these remain in the Fancy very long, unless they learn better, the hard way.

In some instances puppies are acquired from pet shops, stray dogs' homes, or from one of the other sources, either without a certificate of vaccination, or after so-called vaccination with an unreliable product.

It is advisable to isolate such puppies for 3 weeks before submitting them to vaccination, and to vaccinate them then only if they show no symptoms, or not more than a very slight rise in temperature, which might reasonably be attributed to excitement. Apart from the fact that vaccination at the time of purchase might fail to prevent the development of the disease in a puppy already infected, thus bringing the vaccine unfairly into disrepute, there is no evidence that the injection of vaccine into a puppy incubating the disease has any ill effect upon its chances of recovery.

Vaccines, according to their method of manufacture may contain in the same dose, protection against distemper alone, or may protect also against virus hepatitis and leptospiral jaundice. Hardpad is not a separate disease but merely a particular type of distemper.

The use of the multiple vaccine is worth the additional cost since virus hepatitis seems to be even more prevalent at times and in certain localities than distemper, and although it varies a good deal in symptoms and severity, it may prove to be a very fatal disease.

In its mildest form, virus hepatitis may produce rise of temperature, loss of appetite, and diarrhoea. At other times it may give rise to initial vomiting followed by severe haemorrhage from stomach and intestine, and often death within 48 hours. In the most severe form in puppies, sudden deaths may occur.

Leptospiral jaundice is usually caught from rat infection or from eating biscuit or other food upon which an infected rat has voided urine. It can take two forms: one is associated with kidney destruction, while the other gives rise to liver disease and jaundice. Either type may be contracted by human beings.

A measles virus now in fairly frequent use is claimed to prevent the multiplication of distemper virus in the body of the puppy. It is in general use in many of the large trading kennels, and protects the puppies until they can be sold.

The main difficulty is determining how long the immunity lasts. Probably it lasts a considerable time, and it is claimed by the manufacturers that there is no liklihood that it may interfere with vaccination by distemper vaccine in the way that the colostrum of an immune bitch may neutralise a virus vaccine; in fact, the measles and distemper vaccine may even be injected at the same time.

It is claimed that measles vaccine will produce immunity against distemper from the 3rd week of life to some undetermined age. It is advisable, however, to reinforce the immunity by the use of distemper vaccine not later than the 9th month.

The immunity conferred either by an egg-adapted or tissue vaccine takes some little while, maybe a month, to reach its optimum efficiency, and until this is established a dog or puppy may be susceptible to a field virus from an ailing dog, from a soiled lamp-post, or a contaminated food utensil. The virus can be brought home on contaminated shoes or clothing.

8

Some Hereditary Conditions Lethal and Sublethal

It is not proposed in this chapter to deal with the many hereditary conditions that result in death at or soon after birth, or with those abnormalities that necessitate destruction. For the moment, we will consider a number of specific features that could eventually wipe out a breed or make it uneconomical to maintain.

The factor most likely to encourage such faults in any breed is the persistence of a minority of breeders to refuse to recognise that such faults exist, preferring to blindfold their eyes and maintain they have never observed them.

Some of these defects are not confined to a particular breed; in fact, the same fault may appear in totally dissimilar breeds, but the hereditary tendency is present and it is advisable that every breeder should do his or her utmost to eliminate such tendencies before they damage the breed irretrievably.

In spite of generations of selective breeding, each 'pure-bred' dog has as many different types in its extended pedigree as any despised mongrel.

It is true that no genes are handed down unless they have existed in the genetic make-up of its parents. A breeding pair may carry few or many different genes but the total number within the pair is fixed precisely and cannot be increased.

There is, therefore, a definite limit to what a breeder is able to produce, good or bad, from one pair of dogs. It is possible to fix a strain but not to endow any of its members with characteristics not already existent in the parents.

Sometimes luck in breeding would appear to depend upon the characteristics that can be lost rather than upon those that can be gained. Each puppy inherits half its genes from the sire and half from the dam, and these genes, one from each parent, come together at fertilisation to form the fertilised egg containing a sample of each parent's inheritance. The influence of grandparents as regards any specific characteristic diminishes 50 per cent with each succeeding generation. Eventually each g.g.g. grandparent contributes $3\frac{1}{8}$ per cent to every one of its progeny. No more than a single pair of genes can be present on their loci on a single pair of chromosomes. If multiple inheritance is involved, still only two genes can be present, but any two of a number. Some characteristics are controlled by a single pair of genes, while others are controlled by a complex of two or more pairs.

For example, we may consider coat colour. Black, red, and white are controlled by a single pair in each case but there may be present a complex of other genes controlling inhibitors, diluents, etc., which modify the simple inheritance and produce such colours as silver or apricot, and many other shades.

The whole subject of genetics is only truly understood by the few (which does not include the writer) and I would like to quote a remark made to me by my esteemed friend, Commander Norman Hinton, who defined a skilled stockbreeder as 'one who has made lucky guesses based on scientific theories which are imperfectly understood'.[1]

In the development of a breed to conform with an accepted standard, the concentration of genes of a like pattern becomes more pronounced, and this accounts for the greater number of abnormalities in dogs bred to attain a single pattern than in mongrels which breed more or less promiscuously into blood lines entirely different from their own, although even in mongrels hereditary faults may occasionally make an appearance.

Apart from certain well-known specific defects that have been written about a great deal already, there are still

[1] The reader is recommended to read *Practical Dog Breeding and Genetics*, Popular Dogs Publishing Co.

many conditions that crop up fairly frequently but are seldom discussed, although they have a very definite existence and often cause puppy deaths at an early age.

These may involve the digestive system, the respiratory system, or the blood vessels and circulation, and it is just as important to look out for and recognise these hereditary defects as it is to worry about progressive retinal atrophy, hip dysplasia, or slipping patella.

Taking the digestive system first, it is surprising how many puppies the veterinary surgeon sees, destined to die from inability to swallow milk or food, digest it when swallowed, or eliminate it from the bowel after it has been digested.

Inability to swallow food may arise from abnormality of the oesophagus. This defect is far more common than one would suppose, since many puppies die in the first week of life from sheer starvation, and the cause is seldom inquired into.

The common abnormalities associated with the oesophagus, which conveys food from the mouth to the stomach, are stricture or dilation, or both together in different parts of the same oesophagus.

The oesophagus may be too long, giving rise to a 'kink' just before it passes through the diaphragm (the partition between thorax and abdomen). Sometimes there is a stricture (a narrowing of the lumen) at this point or even higher up in the tube, but even more frequently the oesophagus becomes trapped within the thorax between the curvature of the arch of the aorta (the main arterial blood vessel) as it leaves the heart, and a ligament that holds the aorta in place.

This causes difficulty in swallowing or makes it impossible for food to reach the stomach. The oesophagus becomes dilated in front of the stricture, and although operation may relieve the pressure on the oesophagus, it cannot reduce the dilation, hence recovery is seldom complete.

Another site of obstruction, this time to the passage of food out of the stomach (sometimes seen in more than one member of the litter), is due to a constriction of the pylorus, the outlet of the stomach. This is also seen in children and may be remedied in many instances by operation.

Usually, in the larger breeds, but occasionally even in small breeds such as Pugs (and we have seen it on one occasion each in a Yorkshire Terrier and a Dachshund), the stomach may rotate out of its normal position after a meal. The stomach fills with gas and, failing an emergency operation the dog may suffocate through abdominal pressure and heart failure. This can happen quite early in life.

In other cases puppies go into fresh homes, and for the first few days are fed at irregular intervals by various members of the family. They become distended with gas, and die either from suffocation or diarrhoea. In the earlier stages some well-meaning friend may diagnose worms and run to the chemist for a remedy. That is often the end of the story. Not a hereditary fault but one to guard against.

Inability to suck The puppy is directed to its mother's teat by body gyrations brought about by the front end of the body moving through an oval space, the fixed part being the puppy's buttocks, with almost (at this age) useless hind limbs.

But the puppy may have a hare lip or a cleft palate or it may lack ability to hold the teat in the mouth long enough to extract sufficient nourishment. Sometimes the teats of the bitches, instead of being pointed (convex) are concave and difficult to grip in the mouth.

At other times the puppy may lack scent discrimination and fail to find the teat as it can neither see it nor smell it.

Telescoping the bowel (intussusception) may occur when there is excessive bowel movement, arising from indigestion or during diarrhoea. The bowel slips into the adjoining following portion and forms a double layer, the bowel surfaces quickly uniting to produce an immediate bowel obstruction, terminating in gangrene of the imprisoned piece of bowel, and early death. Since this tendency towards intussusception seems particularly prevalent in certain breeds (Irish Setters and Cairns are two of them) it is just possible that there is a hereditary tendency.

Hernia Various types occur in puppies and usually become more marked as the puppy grows. Umbilical hernia, at the navel, is hereditary and may cause death at or just before birth through prolapse of intestine through the aperture, but more often it causes no trouble unless the overlying skin is torn. These cases are readily 'cured' by operation but such individuals should not be bred from.

Inguinal hernia in the groin is fairly common in bitch puppies, notably in toys and in Poodles (perhaps because there are so many Poodles).

The uterus is supported by a wide band of peritoneum attached to the pelvic roof. This 'broad ligament', as it is termed, gives off a thin fibrous band which passes through the inguinal canal in the groin and is attached at one side of the vulva of the bitch. In inguinal hernia, this band (the round ligament of the uterus), draws the uterine horn down into the hernia. In the pregnant bitch the hernia may contain one or more puppies.

Congenital luxation of joints is common in all breeds especially in the small varieties. Elbows, slipping patella and other similar conditions are well known. In black Toy Poodles, an inability to extend one or both hind limbs may occur, associated with contraction of certain tendons, apart from a somewhat similar appearance produced by slipping patella.

In some breeds, notably in Bostons, a 'double-jointed' condition is not uncommonly seen at birth, and such puppies are known as 'swimmers' because their arms are extended laterally and their hind limbs appear weak, so that the puppy does not stand but crawls about on its stomach. Many puppies, so affected, become normal by the third month of life if persevered with.

Rickets is another condition, often hereditary in the sense that the body mechanism regulating the absorption and retention of calcium is abnormal. In other words, a co dition indistinguishable from rickets may appear in a litter even when nutritional features are normal.

Inability to defaecate It is not rare for a puppy to live and suck for 2 to 3 weeks without passing any motion. The body swells, and on examination no anus can be found. Some cases respond to operation. In others, the sphincter of the anus is unable to relax and no faeces are passed.

Even when these cases respond to operation the survivors should never be bred from.

9

Rearing and Temperament

A dog of excellent conformation may be, or should be, regarded as useless for exhibition purposes, if it is nervous of all two-legged creatures, or ring-shy. Even if by some fortunate or unfortunate chance it gets one day into the money it should never be bred from since timidity is just as much a hereditary condition as entropion, or a butterfly nose.

On the other hand, when a dog that is good in all other respects lies down in the ring or bites the judge, one may wonder whether the trouble originates from its breeding or its ownership.

There are three possible influences at work, and the importance of each may vary in individual cases. These are (*a*) heredity, (*b*) environment, (*c*) education.

That heredity influences temperament is indicated by the fact that certain breeds show a general tendency either towards an affection for and a dependence upon humanity in general and to one person in particular; or their members may exhibit a degree of wariness ranging from distrust to aggressiveness, directed against all comers, human or otherwise.

There may be individual differences in each breed but on the whole there is a definite breed tendency towards some particular type of temperament.

Marca Burns and Margaret N. Fraser, in a recent edition of their book *Genetics of the Dog* (Oliver and Boyd Edinburgh), discuss significant differences between breeds in susceptibility to fear which were experienced by Mahut (1958) when investigating the initial reactions of 210 normally reared pure-bred dogs of ten breeds, to a number of innocuous strange objects.

In the 'fearful' group came Collies, Alsatians, Poodles, Corgis and Dachshunds. The 'fearless' group, showing avoidance of teasing and approach, comprised Boxers, Boston, Bedlington, and Scottish Terriers.

Mahut also compared the reactions of unrelated dogs of these breeds when reared in kennels with those of similar dogs raised in a home amid human society.

He found that while the home-reared Scotties and Boxers were fearless and even aggressive, each breed exhibiting its own pattern of response, those kept in kennels were more timid or fearful, and the pattern of their responses no longer differed.

Some of the more fearsome-looking breeds such as Bulldogs and Bull mastiffs may be the gentlest of creatures, while a Pekingese or a Yorkshire Terrier may be extremely ferocious in its own small way.

There would appear to be two types of aggressive behaviour: (*a*) an active desire to attack any animals, including man, (*b*) a varying degree of fear of mankind, other animals and certain strange objects, with a tendency to snap, or bite, as a means of defence, coupled with a desire to escape. The latter may take priority and the natural weapons may come into use only when they aid escape, impossible without their employment.

Every dog, like most other animals, has an 'escape distance', in other words an ability to estimate its own power to escape from another animal. Nor does it permit such an animal to approach beyond the distance compatible with safety, before making a getaway.

In actual fact, very few dogs attack and bite human beings, or other dogs, so long as they do not venture within the dog's own personal territory. Within that territory the proprietor has dominance. A Pekingese may furiously attack an intruding Alsatian and the latter will depart (Fig. 8) without resistance until it has reached the boundaries of the former's territory, when it may put on an entire change of front.

The most difficult thing in training a police dog, an

Alsatian for example, is to make it grip and *hold* a man. Some dogs have no great objection to biting, provided they can bite and run away, but a well-trained police dog should not actually bite, although its jaw grip through clothing may cause bruising. Holding on to the man entails responsibility (some might regard it as a 'lack of conscience') and only a minor percentage of dogs can accomplish this, even after prolonged training. Dogs reared in domestication

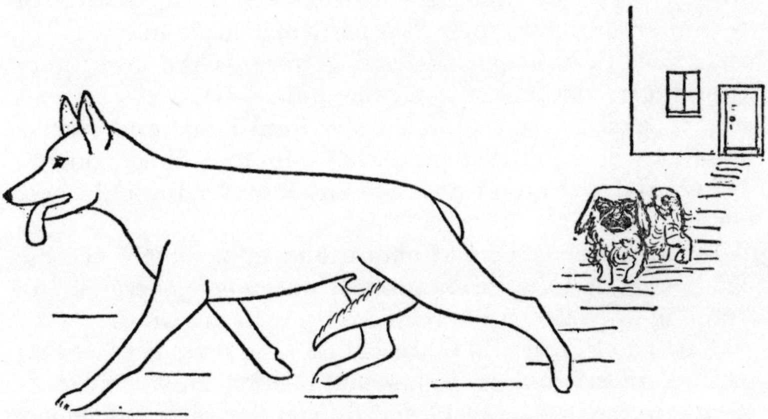

Figure 8 A Pekingese 'seeing off' an intruding Alsatian

under suitable conditions and in sound environment seldom bite except when frightened or hurt, but dogs reared in the wild invariably bite if molested at close quarters.

Neither aggression nor fearfulness are accepted in show dog or pet, if they are pronounced.

While it seems to be an accepted fact that the basic elements of temperament have a genetic origin, it is still hard to decide how much of a dog's behaviour may depend upon the environment in which it has been reared or upon the temperament of the person who has reared it. A great many dogs that are naturally aggressive will submit to a personality more dominant than their own, but may not remain submissive should the human dominance show the slightest sign of weakening.

On the whole, the neurotic owner usually rears a neurotic dog, while the jolly, happy-go-lucky type of owner more often raises puppies with sentiments similar to his own.

Puppies appear to take their cues in the first place from the behaviour of their mother towards persons and animals, which is easy to do if they possess similar genetic features.

If the mother fears strangers of any species the puppies display suspicion and, thereafter, become aggressive or fearful according to their own particular make-up.

In any case, a genetic leaning towards the acceptance of strangers can be lost in a generation.

If a good-tempered bitch strays from home and rears a litter in wild surroundings, all her puppies will fear human beings and will attack and bite any intruder through sheer panic.

Such puppies revert to nature and immediately become wild animals in spite of several preceding generations of training and close social relationship with mankind.

Burns and Fraser, in *Genetics of the Dog*, stress the fact that neither genetic nor environmental factors can act independently in the development and differentiation of behaviour. They consider that, what is extremely important is the age at which socialisation makes its impression, and that there is a critical period in every puppy's life when a small amount of experience will produce a great effect on its future behaviour.

Puppies vary as regards the age at which they begin to 'see' objects, as opposed to cataloguing them according to their odour. After the 3rd week the primary period of socialisation begins when the puppy first begins to notice other individuals.

Experiments show that Alsatians rank highest at this stage, and Poodles lowest. Between the 3rd and 4th weeks the presence of the mother is necessary to reassure the puppy, and if for any reason the mother has to be removed from her litter during these seven days it has a bad effect on the confidence displayed by the puppies, and this lack of confidence may persist into adult life.

If the puppy is to grow into a well-adjusted dog, it must also experience socialisation with other puppies at this period.

The character of the dog is formed between three and sixteen weeks.

Pfaffenberger is quoted as saying, from his experience of guide dog training, that however good the inherited character traits may be, if they are not given opportunity for expression before the age of sixteen weeks, the dog will never be as good as it might have become. It will be poor material for any form of training, and its ability to adapt itself to human companionship will be limited. It may become either a bully or an underdog. Disciplined training must definitely be given between twelve and sixteen weeks.

Apparently some breeds are more affected by the process of socialisation with human beings than others.

At five weeks Basenjis, which are more akin to the wild dog than most other developed breeds, begin to exhibit timidity, more so than either Beagles or Wire-haired Terriers, but as they become socialised the timidity of all three breeds becomes much less.

Some breeds appear to be born socialised to humanity—the result of heredity—but the writer doubts whether this would apply to a litter of, let us say, Cocker Spaniels, born in the wild and not having been accustomed to the sight of human beings from soon after the opening of their eyes.

In this connection 'imprinting', as described by Konrad Lorenz, must be given consideration.

He showed that a dog, or any trainable animal, accepted the first human being upon which it set eyes, as a parent figure, and given the opportunity, would devote itself to that person throughout its life, regarding itself as a member of the pack with its accepted parent figure as 'pack boss'. Lorenz was referring to puppies in domestication, not to those born wild.

Ability to accept responsibility is primarily an inherent temperamental characteristic that can be strengthened by education and affected by environment.

In training bitches to lead the blind, many will do well and pass all tests until asked to lead a blindfolded handler. They may then become confused and lose confidence since this necessitates an acceptance of responsibility that may be more than the canine mind can visualise.

Nearly all of those that fail in this test have entailed a temporary loss of social relationship at the critical period of their lives. Any emotional disturbance between the ages of three and sixteen weeks can completely disarrange the temperament and character for the rest of the dog's life. A sense of responsibility was more easily acquired by bitch puppies if they were given training between eight and ten weeks, then taken to a foster home and reared in the midst of human family until twelve months old, when training was resumed.

The puppy's education depends largely upon trial and error and the recollection of types of behaviour response that have brought unpleasant repercussions. The puppy learns to connect the behaviour with the type of reception it receives.

At a year old it knows all the answers, with suitable responses as judged by *human* standards, and it will have grown familiar with the many forms of stimuli it will be likely to encounter in the human family circle.

A child takes twenty years or more to acquire the relative degree of intelligence displayed by the average dog at twelve months.

Genetics of the Dog: the Basis of Successful Breeding, by Marca Burns and Margaret Fraser (Oliver & Boyd, Edinburgh), is a book every lover of dogs should read. It is priced at 45*s*. but to those who regard breeding dogs as a scientific pursuit rather than as a hit-and-miss gamble, it will be worth every penny of it; also, *Practical Dog Breeding and Genetics*, by Dr Eleanor Frankling, Popular Dogs Publishing Co., London.

10

The Pick of the Litter

We breed litters for two reasons. One is to produce and retain an exceptionally good specimen either for future exhibition, or as a valuable asset to our own breeding stock. The other is that breeding and maintaining a kennel is a very expensive business and it is only by the 'lucky chance' and our ability to sell our surplus puppies at a respectable price that we can shoo the wolf from our door and remain a little longer in the Fancy.

If the sale of surplus puppies is to enable us to pay our way it is essential to maintain a very high breeding standard; quality rather than quantity. We shall also be obliged to dispose of to friends and competitors a good many puppies we would have preferred to keep had the economic situation been easier. The breeding of rubbish 'good enough for the pet market', not only degrades dog breeding in general, but it also deprives the honest, ambitious breeder of a potential market, one very much needed in order to make both ends meet.

Knowing which puppy or puppies to retain and which to sell from a good, level litter is not easy unless one pays careful regard to certain basic factors that can readily be learned.

One cannot but admire the 'old hand' who claims the ability to spot the pick of the litter on the 3rd day, the 3rd week or the 3rd month, but all breeders do not possess this gift and many who do might find it beyond them to explain the why and the wherefore of their decisions.

To those who have some slight understanding of the anatomy of the dog, combined with a knowledge of the points of the particular breed, it is a comparatively easy matter at, say, the third day after birth (and much easier later) to separate the 'possibles' from the 'also-rans', purely upon the conformation of the puppy's skeleton. This shows to the trained eye various characteristics unlikely to alter, whatever else occurs during the progress of growth.

Two main factors may play a part in our final selection, or may temper our decision to retain or dispose of any particular puppy at about eight to ten weeks of age, when safely weaned. The first of these is the puppy's conformation. The second is its temperament.

It might seem to be difficult to get an insight into the possible temperament of the adult dog from the behaviour of a puppy between three and six weeks but there are many indications if one knows how to recognise them. When newborn puppies lie wriggling in a heap, the development of a social hierarchy is already on its way.

Within a few hours No. 1 has staked its claim in its mother's groin—the warmest site—and is busily sucking the terminal teat. Close up, alongside, will be Nos. 2 and 3 hanging on to their chosen teats or nudging each other off at every opportunity, but at the same time maintaining a good position at the milk-bar and keeping comfortably warm.

Travelling forward along the line of puppies we finally come to the less lusty members and, at the terminus, there may be one that sucks but little, and feels cold. This individual may receive little or no attention from its mother, especially when it carries the 'sick smell'. Some bitches will push it out. The natural human sympathy will tend to cosset this puppy and attempt to rear it away from the rest. The genes for survival appear to be distributed very unevenly and with a view to the ultimate stamina of a strain, nature's plan for the survival of the fittest still deserves every respect.

Even after the eyes open, the 'sucking order' is retained and it is not until the 18th day (sometimes the 20th) that vision plays any great part in a puppy's activities. At this date it begins to distinguish between still and moving objects. At first, moving bodies are reflected in the mirror of the eyes as shadows which draw nearer to fixed objects, or recede from them, or even dart across the mirror. The ability to associate these images within the eye with disturbances 'in space', outside the puppy's body, develops earlier and more rapidly in some individuals of a litter than in others, and may be accepted as an index of future intelligence.

If one approaches a three-week-old litter very quietly and carefully, one may observe that while the majority appear unconcerned and lethargic, troubling little to use their eyes, one of the puppies may display eye movements, apparently watching the incomer with a degree of interest.

Later, it may often be noticed that this puppy is usually the first to rouse itself and come forward to meet the visitor who brings the pan of milk, or will watch which finger-tip is smeared with scraped, raw beef.

It is also frequently the first to demonstrate its presence vocally. In a great many instances, by colour, markings and sex, it will be discovered that this was the puppy that grabbed the best teat directly after birth.

Such a puppy is more likely to associate its own existence with that of its human guardian and to provide evidence of what Konrad Lorenz terms 'imprinting'.

It will make man's best companion, regarding itself not as an inferior but as an active member of the family pack, apt to regard other dogs as inferior beings and most willing at all times to live in social amity with acceptable members of the human race.

Unfortunately, most judges find it easier to recognise good conformation, and award marks for it, than to spot and reward excellence of temperament. The two do not always go together and when the two are in separate scale-pans, it is invariably conformation that tips the scale.

It is as well, therefore, that it is a comparatively easy matter to forecast the future outline of the dog by a careful study of the infant skeleton. If we are fortunate enough to find that the puppy exhibiting early intelligence and a liking for human society shows a corresponding grade of conformation lying ahead, there will be no hesitation in deciding upon 'the pick of the litter'.

However, all breeders are of necessity gamblers and are quite aware that the jackpot is a very slippery little article. After all, if success in breeding came easily to all of us, our interest in it would cease.

We talk about even, level litters, but in point of fact we seldom encounter one. Nor it is to be expected, except on odd occasions.

Each puppy carries a number of genes, each devoted or partially so, to some characteristic, obtained from both its parents. The influence of grandparents as regards any specific characteristic diminishes by 50 per cent with each succeeding generation.

Those genes imparted to it by its sire and dam are arranged in groups resembling strings of beads, each string representing a *chromosome*. The chromosomes lie in the nucleus, the central part of the puppy's body cells, and in the ordinary (somatic) cells the chromosomes are arranged in pairs, two of each kind, and it has been estimated that the dog's cells contain thirty-nine chromosome pairs. But in the *reproductive* cells the pairs of chromosomes separate so that each sperm or ovum contains only *one* of each pair of chromosomes.

When mating occurs between dog and bitch and when a sperm meets an ovum and fuses with it, the number of chromosomes again becomes seventy-eight, the developing puppy receiving *one* chromosome of *each pair* from *each* parent.

But the matter is not so simple as it might appear to be, for the chromosomes exhibit differences in almost every breed.

The individual genes are arranged in set and definite order on the chromosomes and any variation in their position may have a marked effect upon the characteristic they produce. The two genes normally occupy the same relative positions on their chromosomes.

Genes always occur in pairs, one member of the pair on

one chromosome and the other on the partner chromosome. The two genes are *alleles* of each other, whether they have similar or dissimilar influences. The word 'allele' means 'alternative' and when a puppy has not inherited the one gene out of a pair of genes, then it *must* have inherited the other.

The two genes, one from the sire and one from the dam, combine during fertilisation at random, and which sperm fertilises which ovum is purely a matter of chance; herein lies the gamble that makes dog breeding what it is.

The degree of possible variation may be considerably reduced when the mother and father are closely linked genetically, as by in-breeding.

It is obvious, therefore, that identical puppies will not be found in any litter apart from the occasional instance in which two puppies develop from the division of a single ovum.

There are, however, certain features present in each newborn living puppy that will change but little during the period during which the puppy is attaining its adult shape.

It is a fact, however, that certain genes within a puppy may cause some of the long bones to grow abnormally long or to remain abnormally short. But, fortunately, during the course of centuries we have established breeds that, by standard, will grow lengthy limb bones and others that will remain stunted, and it is only when a breed is being developed, as an intermediate, that we are a little uncertain as to how much or how little their bones may grow.

In time, these characteristics become fixed, but in an intermediate breed such as the Boxer, not only limb characteristics but jaw growth and tooth size also, are added to the problem.

The majority of the basic breeds now follow a fairly calculable pattern of development and a study of the skeletal structure of the newborn puppy should provide a very good indication of its subsequent conformation provided that one is closely familiar with the breed, and conversant with the standard laid down for the particular variety.

There are a number of points which will require study and one will need to bear in mind the diverse characters present in each of the separate breeds that may have gone into the construction of a new variety. This is particularly evident when considering puppies of intermediate type, when for example a variety contains unknown fractions of dolichocephalic (long-headed) and brachycephalic (short-headed) ancestry.

In order to discuss the characteristics of newborn puppies it will help if we pick three typical but diverse breeds and compare the characteristics to which special attention might be paid in each.

Let us select:

(*a*) Smooth Fox Terrier;
(*b*) Cocker Spaniel;
(*c*) Pekingese.

In most varieties certain basic characteristics are present common to all, with others peculiar to the breed.

Some of these we can discuss are:

1 Head shape;
2 Limb length;
3 Chest capacity;
4 Body length;
5 Angulation.

At this stage we may mention general appearance. Colour is not always easy to decide from that apparent at birth. Blacks may become blue, as in Kerries. White may become spotted or ticked. Dalmatians are always white at birth, apart from occasional patches, the spots appearing later. Ticking, as seen in Setters and Spaniels, may not be visible in the newborn. In white Bull Terriers ticking may be present at birth and disappear within a few weeks. It is interesting to note whether dark hairs correspond with pigmented areas of skin immediately surrounding their roots. Eyelid pigmentation, as in white Poodles, is usually visible at birth although it may not completely encircle the eye at this age. Pink noses may evidence themselves at birth but are not to be discarded too early if they show scattered spots of pigmentation. Cleft palate may not always be evident until the puppy sucks and milk comes down the nostrils.

The anus should always be examined soon after birth to ensure that it is open and capable of passing faeces. It is not unknown for a puppy to live as long as 14 to 16 days, growing larger in the abdomen, and when examined by an expert it may be found that it has an imperforate anus and has never passed faeces. Kinked tails are visible soon after birth.

Ear placement and leather size can be judged fairly well at a very early age. Markings are usually recognisable in the newborn. The head markings of a Boston do not change a great deal from those with which the puppy is born. Eye size and shape can usually be foretold by the 2nd or 3rd week. The round pop-eye never becomes almond shape (even if the almond eye may finish up completely round).

THE HEAD

There are three main portions of the skull. Firstly, the cranium centrally situated, which contains the brain; secondly, the orbit (surrounded by the zygomatic arch of bone containing the eyeball); and thirdly, the upper and lower jaws. We may observe these three main features in the head of the newborn puppy, whatever the breed. In the Chihuahua feel, too, for the presence of a *Molero*, a gap in the central portion of the cranium immediately above the 'stop'. This can be felt with the finger-tip, through the skin. The main features to be examined in the young puppy are (*a*) width of skull (*b*) length (*c*) the jaws. In each of the three breeds under consideration (Cocker, Smooth

Fox Terrier, and Pekingese) skull width is quite different, and this is of first importance.

The present width is determined quite simply, and the future width is estimated by carefully feeling between the tips of the fingers the bony structure known as the *zygomatic arch* (described later, *see* Fig. 9). The results must then be compared in the individual members of each litter. The degree of zygomatic curvature is fixed genetically at birth and no degree of massage or other treatment will alter its shape one iota.

The Fox Terrier puppies

In these, as in the other two breeds being considered, one must be able to recognise and palpate with the finger tips the whole length of the zygoma and the degree of curvature in its arch.

The zygomatic arch is formed by a rather solid arc of bone extending from the opening by which the ear canal enters the skull, in an outward and forward direction. It thus encloses and encircles the eyeball (and provides this with a good deal of protection). Travelling forwards and slightly downwards, the zygoma rejoins the skull at a point below the eye socket, just above the spot occupied below the cheek by the 'carnassial', the large cheek tooth in the adult (*see* Fig. 10).

The curvature giving rise to the arch of the zygoma also affords protection to the cranium which encloses the brain. At its upper end between the zygoma and the cranium, the zygomatic arch gives passage to the upper end of the lower jaw and during opening and closing of the mouth as in chewing or barking, the jawbone can be felt moving freely within its curvature. In Fox Terrier puppies the zygoma must be free from arching and almost parallel with the side of the skull, leaving only just enough space in the orbit (between the zygoma and the cranium) to contain the eye-ball in front and the upper end of the lower jaw behind.

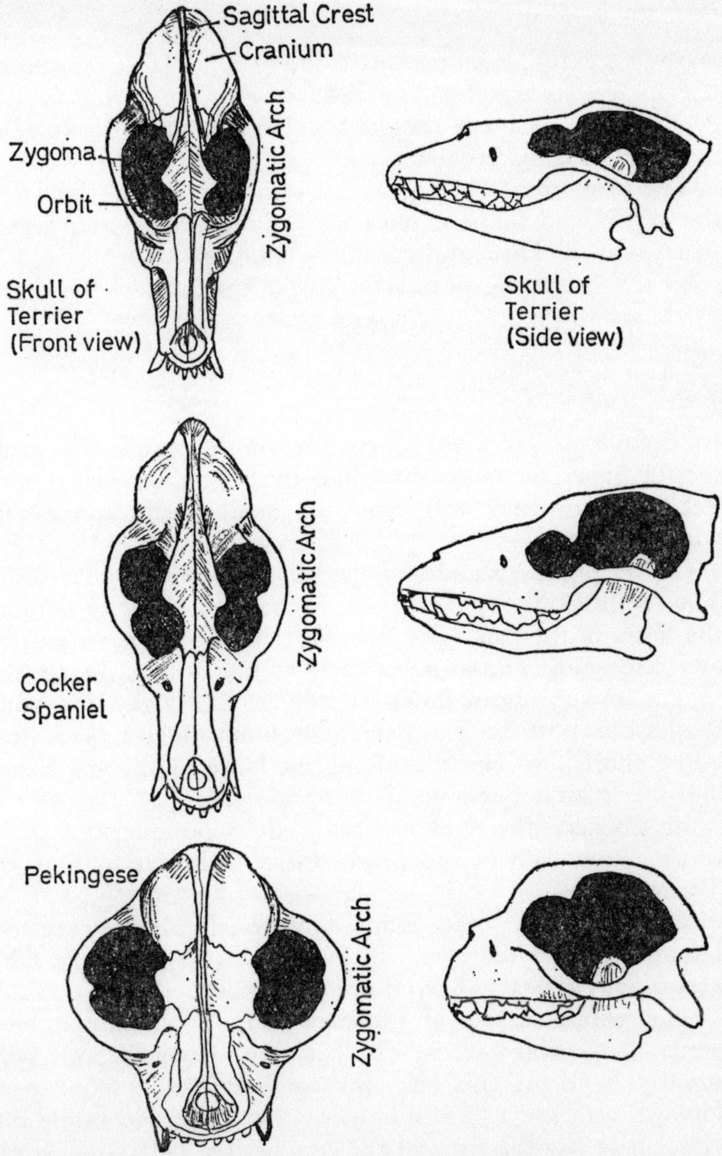

Figure 9 Dogs' skulls showing zygomatic arches and orbits

Pekingese puppies

With a Pekingese puppy it is important before anything else to feel its weight. The Peke is a compact dog and a good puppy at birth should feel heavier than one would imagine, judging from its size.

The head must be big, with width and flatness between the ears. Head shape is more easily judged now than later, when skin thickness and coat may confuse.

In the Pekingese puppy the finger tip can feel the zygomatic arch practically as a semicircle.

Spaniel puppies

In Spaniel puppies the curvature of the zygomatic arch should never be more than half that seen, or felt, in the Pekingese, or they will grow up 'skully' with too much width of cheek.

Cocker puppies should also present well-developed *occiputs*. The occiput is the highest point of the skull above or behind the bases of the ears. The Fox Terriers should have hardly any discernible curvature of the zygoma so that the cheeks lie flat and the head flows laterally in a straight line from ear base to nostrils. The Pekingese should have a deep stop and a short jaw. The eyes should be large by the 3rd week, and moderately prominent—not pop-eyed.

In Cockers, the eyes are set a little obliquely, a little to the outer side of the head, but a little less so than in Terriers.

The ears of a Terrier follow the eyes. If the eyes are too laterally placed the ears will follow suit. Well-carried ears accompany a nearly-frontal eye placement.

The potential size of the ears can be estimated more easily at the third week. The best Fox Terrier puppy will usually have, at this age, the smallest ears, placed well forward and not at the side of the head. Within limits the closer together the roots of the ears lie, the better the head. Wide cheeks go with laterally-placed ears.

In Cockers, pick the puppy with ears set low upon the side of the head, leaving a clean, domed skull above and between their points of insertion into the skull.

The Pekingese is the most difficult of the three breeds to pick, on account of its head, as in the brachycephalic heads there are so many diverse factors to consider. The size of the head is a help, but the degree of stop, wrinkling and jaw placements are more variable in these dogs during growth than in the long-headed types. Cleft palate must be looked for soon after birth.

The potential jaw length is often made predictable in the Spaniel and Terrier by relating it to the (lack of) width of zygomatic arches.

When these show marked curvature at an early age there is little hope of a head developing in keeping with the requirements of the standard.

Undershot jaws are usually recognisable at a very early age and, generally speaking, in the long-headed breeds a very slightly overshot jaw is a far safer bet. Growth in the lower jaw is almost invariably faster and carries on longer than in the upper jaw, and it is fairly safe to expect the jaw the least bit undershot at birth to develop into a typically undershot jaw at, or before, maturity.

THE NECK AND SHOULDERS

The length of a dog's neck may decide whether it jogs along on the road to fame or stays in its kennel. But what would be ideal in one breed might be quite wrong in another. Our Fox Terrier and our Cocker choice will need to have long necks. In their future life they will both have to exercise a great deal of head movement which would be impossible if the necks were short and their lower ends squeezed in between the two scapulae.

In nine cases out of ten the short, cramped neck goes in company with upright scapulae (shoulder blades). So, when looking over your Terrier and Cocker puppies pick those with long necks and sloping scapulae, that is, with shoulders which at their upper extremities lie well back upon the dorsal bones.

The degree of inclination of the scapula will be just as positive or negative at the third day of life as at the third month. It is a fixed characteristic and inborn. A bad, upright shoulder never corrects itself, but it may become worse, especially when exercise is limited and the puppy too well fed.

We may now take another look at our litter of Pekingese. The standard says nothing about the length of neck desirable in the breed but one may presume that it would not be noticeably long in a variety furnished with a thick-set body. A particularly lengthy neck in a Pekingese owning a large round head, might produce a rather grotesque result if the head could be protruded and cocked at a variety of angles. Nor does the Pekingese standard say anything about the layback of shoulder but it does insist upon absolute soundness and forelegs firm at the shoulder, so it may be presumed that in this breed we may expect to see a moderately inclined shoulder accompanied by a rather sturdy, compact neck. These characteristics may be recognised, or markedly absent, in the Pekingese puppy as early as the third week and it is rather unlikely that as regards the relative proportion between neck and shoulders the puppy will undergo any marked change as it grows.

CHEST CAPACITY

All three of the breeds under consideration require depth of chest but the actual shape of the chest is a little different in each of the three breeds (Terriers, Cockers, and Pekingese). In a Fox Terrier the chest will require depth and width without being in any way barrel-shaped. In the young puppy, while apparent depth is good, it may be as well to plump for the well-filled chest of good capacity rather than for one that is too flat-sided, and may stay that way. The ribs take weeks or months to lengthen, and the sternum (breast bone) seldom reaches down to the level of the elbows before the puppy is at least six months old. In the Cockers, the ribs are stouter than in the Terriers and develop more rapidly, and the sternum reaches its low level somewhat earlier. In spite of this, up to six or eight weeks of age it is safer to give marks for chest capacity rather than for chest shape. The tendency is always for the final shape to be that common in the breed.

LENGTH OF BODY

Right from the time of birth in almost every breed it is possible to get a fairly correct estimate of the final length of the body by measuring the space between the last rib and the stifle joint. Even when the ribs extend well backward (as they should do), the body will still be short provided this space is short. The puppy may have a particularly long (not necessarily strong) loin, which may account for the appearance of length. At any rate, a short back cannot be associated with a long gap between the last rib and the stifle. All three of our breeds must correspond in this respect.

LOIN

Strength or weakness of the muscles of the loin may be apparent even before these have been submitted to any appreciable amount of exercise. Muscle volume becomes evident at quite an early age. In the running breeds, Greyhounds, Afghans, Salukis, and the like, the muscle mass is relatively greater than in the Shepherd breeds such as the Alsatian, in which muscle volume over the loins and quarters has been reduced in order to effect a lowering of the hindquarters coupled with exaggerated angulation. Although hip dysplasia is rarely present at the time of birth the conformation which predisposes to it may be visible, and it is now stated by some authorities that the incidence of the disease in the fully grown dog bears a direct relationship to the presence or absence of potential muscle mass over the loin and pelvis at the time of birth. This theory does not meet with general acceptance. It is seldom that whole litters are affected with dysplasia and although we may be deliberately departing from the approved type we would probably be doing the right thing in selecting the puppy with strong, well-muscled loins and quarters, regardless as to whether this lessened the degree of angulation, at this early age.

THE LIMBS

It is not always easy in the newly born puppy to foresee how the limbs may finally develop but one can usually decide whether they are likely to finish up long or short. This applies especially to such breeds as the Greyhound and the Scottish Terrier, in each of which the pattern is now so firmly established that it is unlikely they will deviate to any marked degree so far as length is concerned.

This regularity of conformation was not the result of selective breeding or of the ingenuity of man in the first place, but was due to a mutation which involved certain ductless glands within the body with changes in the output or hormones, or in the hormones themselves, and it is these changes that have brought about corresponding changes in the shapes of these particular breeds, and of many others, ranging from the short-faced breeds such as the Bulldog and Griffon to the long-headed varieties such as the Afghan and Saluki.

The limb bones of the newly born puppy are composed mainly of cartilage; the mineral contents, which provide rigidity, being deposited in the cartilage as the puppy develops and grows.

The limbs have to support the puppy from the 3rd week of life, and according to the amount of mineral substances deposited in the cartilage, together with the weight of the body and the degree of activity displayed by the puppy, so will the bones of the limbs, particularly the forelimbs, remain straight or adopt a degree of curvature.

There is undoubtedly also a genetic 'rickety' tendency

towards bone curvature but whether this is dependent upon the amount of mineral deposited, or upon the original shape of the foundation cartilage, is not clear.

In some breeds a moderate degree of bone curvature is accepted as normal, while it would be regarded as unsoundness in others.

In those breeds in which curvature is demanded it will be visible in the cartilaginous limb at the time of birth or very soon after, and it may also be evident in the limbs of other breeds that require straight limbs but are about to become 'rickety'.

In breeds requiring straight bone, such as most of the long-limbed Terriers, any visible degree of curvature would bring about their rejection, and so the tendency is for these breeds to produce straight bone as the result of selective breeding.

At the same time it must be remembered that many breeds of Terriers have been bred larger than their original ancestors, which had shorter legs essential to their mode of life, living, as they did, mainly among rocks and in rough country and catching much of their food by going to ground to fetch it.

Today, one of these short-legged dogs with curved limbs will reappear in a fashionable litter from time to time, causing much consternation. Such a puppy might well be used to reproduce the original Terrier as a new breed instead of being disposed of with a reverend title to which it has no claim.

The bones that mainly adopt a curve are the radius and ulna of the forelimb but another abnormality that is becoming more frequent in certain breeds, notably Terriers and Afghans, is a bending outwards of the forelimb below the carpus (knee joint), amounting in some cases to a subluxation or mild type of dislocation. Some authorities regard this abnormality as being, in a sense, sex-linked, in that it seems to affect either the males or the females in a litter, but seldom both sexes.

Other bone and joint abnormalities, such as slipping patella, cannot always be detected easily in the very young puppy as they appear at a certain stage of growth and by adult age have either become more marked, or may have disappeared provided there is not a marked structural abnormality in the bones involved.

ANGULATION

The degree of angulation required between the scapula and humerus, essential to the well laid-back shoulder, has already been discussed. In the hind limbs, marked angulation demands an exaggerated length of the tibia and a shortening of the limb below the hock joint.

In Alsatian puppies, for instance, a comparison of the length of each puppy from stifle to hock, making due allowance for size and weight of the respective individual, will show definitely which puppy will 'cover the most ground' at maturity. The lengthening of the tibia will coincide with a corresponding shortening of the limb from hock to ground.

It is true that any puppy may alter in shape considerably during the various growth stages, but when the additional tibial length can be recongised during the first few weeks of life, there need be no doubt concerning the degree of angulation that will be attained by the time the puppy becomes adult.

II

Canine Nutrition

Normally the problem of dog feeding is conditioned by the number one keeps; a pack of hounds must be fed with greater regard to economy than a single pet.

The basic requirements of all individuals are similar, whatever their station in life. The main difference lies in the amount of energy the dog is required to expend and, somewhat ironically, it is usually the idle lapdog that fares better than the industrious hound.

The fact remains, however, that in the majority of instances, neither is being fed to the best advantage.

GENERAL CONSIDERATIONS

One of the common errors associated with nutrition lies in widely-accepted belief that the so-called carnivorous animals, including the dog family, as well as all animals that kill and eat each other, are essentially meat eaters and should be restricted to a diet of meat whenever circumstances and economical circumstances permit.

The truth is that very few animals can, or ever attempt to, live on meat alone. All of them require a proportion of their diet to be vegetable material if they are to maintain condition and remain fit and reasonably healthy. Although nobody would suggest depriving dogs of meat, it is a mistaken belief among dog breeders that dogs cannot live without a high proportion of animal protein in their diet. This belief has no experimental foundation.

Dr. Walter Schwick, in his well-known book on dog nutrition, quotes Koehn, who composed an all-vegetable ration containing yellow maize meal, wheat shoots and peanut meal as the chief sources of protein, and found that dogs fed on it retained their fitness and health, with a good rate of growth.

Foxes raised on a fur farm where no meat was fed grew as well as those receiving meat and produced furs of equal quality to those from meat-fed foxes.

Research conducted at Wisconsin University several years ago proved that a diet of ground yellow corn, soya bean oil meal, alfalfa meal, cottonseed oil, mineral supplement, niacin and irradiated yeast, was adequate for the growth and maintenance of dogs, although successful reproduction and lactation were achieved only when liver, fish, and certain vitamins of the B group were added as a supplement.

All animals require proteins for body building: carbohydrates for energy, and fat for warmth. It is probable that ill-health, unthriftiness, thinness or over-fatness, are due in dogs not so much to the quantity of food supplies, as to its quality and, particularly, to the relative proportion of its essential ingredients. A great deal of money can be wasted on foods in which the various nutritive elements required by the body are improperly balanced.

The vegetable material consumed by the wild carnivores is seldom gathered first hand from the land, although in their natural native environment Basenjis eat a certain amount of fresh green material, while the Mexican Hairless Dogs actually graze after the manner of goats, and seldom eat meat in their native habitat.

The regular source of the vegetable material consumed in quantity by all the wild carnivora is that contained in the stomach and digestive organs of the animals they kill. This has been partially digested by fermentation set up in the warm interior of the animal by the action of yeasts, bacteria, and natural enzymes. The rumen of a bullock, or a buffalo, is capable of holding up to half a hundredweight or more of this partly digested vegetable food material. Fermented vegetable material obtained from this source is more valuable to the dog than actual flesh, since it contains the essential vitamins and a variety of other food materials unobtainable by the dog from elsewhere.

The dog, fox, or other carnivore, immediately after making its kill rips open the skin of the abdomen and at once devours as much as possible of the rumen contents of a deer or antelope, and in the same way eats the stomach contents of a rabbit, as well as its intestines.

The flesh may be left alone until the animal's vegetarian requirements are satisfied, and it is not unusual for the flesh to remain untouched for several hours longer. It is in this way that carnivorous animals in the wild obtain the bulk of their vitamins, particularly those of the B-complex, together with a number of enzymes, and in all probability a selection of vitamins as yet unrecorded.

Later in the day, or even after a couple of days if it has not been forestalled, the predator will return and eat part of the victim's liver, melt, lungs or kidneys, all of which contain essential vitamins. Flesh is often left until it is partly decomposed, when it is likely to contain other substances useful to the dog.

A rather interesting story centres around the sheepdogs living on certain hill farms and used entirely for herding sheep on the higher ranges.

When myxomatosis first broke out and the rabbits temporarily disappeared, many of these dogs began to waste away, and many died. It was immediately presumed that the dogs were ill because they were deprived of rabbit flesh, as without this they were fed only ground barley, maize meal, and pig swill. The fact was, however, that few of these dogs ate the flesh of a single rabbit in a month, but they did consume the entrails of all of those that were systematically trapped or shot and gutted on the hills before being taken off the farm. These rabbit entrails had provided the greater part of the dogs' vitamins.

On the lower pastures where the cows grazed, the cattle dogs remained fit and healthy although they had also lost their rabbits. The reason was that they had learned to eat dried cowdung, which also contained the same vitamins, and this supplied their requirements. On the higher ground, the sheep pellets were not eaten by the dogs.

Not so many years ago many dog breeders made a habit of visiting the local slaughterhouse or the knacker's yard and bringing home rumen contents, uncleaned tripe, and melt. These were found to be a valuable pick-me-up for dogs that were not thriving or were out of coat, and were particularly useful in keeping showdogs in tip-top condition. Nowadays, slaughterhouse regulations make it difficult or impossible to obtain such material.

FOOD REQUIREMENTS

Although, in theory, the needs of any individual dog can be estimated by the use of charts and tables, it is equally easy to weigh a dog at intervals. Having ascertained the optimum weight of every dog in the kennel when in fit condition and in perfect health it is as well to record this, and then one may decide whether excess weight demands less food, more exercise, or both, loss of weight indicating a need for extra nourishment. It is soon possible to get to know the sort of food each dog requires and thrives best on.

Increased weight may be due to growth, excessive fatness, muscular development, or even to the over-retention of fluid in the tissues. It may also be associated with pregnancy or with pyometra in the bitch, or in either sex with any dropsical condition. In the two latter, the distension is purely abdominal with increased girth and there may even be loss of flesh in other parts of the body.

It is easier to put on weight than to reduce it. A tendency to obesity appears to be hereditary in some strains, especially among bitches. Excessive fat can be gradually reduced in a healthy subject by increasing the amount of exercise and cutting down on carbohydrates and fats. Lack of body fat may sometimes require a veterinary examination to determine the cause.

In a healthy, worm-free dog, the weight may be increased by extra food containing the essential proteins and carbohydrates and fat, plus the necessary minerals, vitamins, and trace elements in the right proportions. The fats may include oils such as cod-liver, halibut, or small amounts of linseed oil. When these oils are administered it is important to add vitamin E to the diet as this vitamin is destroyed by any excess of vitamin A present in the oils.

Exercise needs to be moderated though it must be sufficient to keep the muscles in good trim. Care should be taken to distinguish the abnormally lean dog from one in a state of hard muscular fitness. The lean dog may be very fit and healthy but the over-fat one may be a sick dog in spite of its prosperous appearance.

The energy value of a food is usually expressed in *calories*; another way of showing how much body heat a particular food is capable of producing. A calorie is the unit of heat that will raise the temperature of one cubic centimetre of water one degree Centigrade.

The heat output of the animal at rest, expressed in calories, is known as the basic metabolic rate. As a result of numerous experiments carried out by many investigators it is now accepted that the requirement of a dog weighing 13·5 kilograms (about 26 lb) is 24 calories for each pound body weight per day. A dog of Cocker size, say 25 lb, would therefore (in theory) require 600 calories daily in terms of food.

This figure, however, was worked out using experimental dogs at rest, and allowance must therefore be made in every case with due regard to the amount of exercise or work, and an appropriate number of calories added to the amount. This is where theory and practice are apt to get a little tangled. A sheepdog on the hills may easily travel 20 to 25 miles in a day, but a Pekingese or a Chihuahua might not do a great deal more than that in yards.

Extensive experiments have shown that the requirements of the normal housedog may average 40 calories for every pound of body weight. On 50 calories per lb most of the experimental dogs put on overweight.

What applies to pets and housedogs in general, does not apply to hounds and working dogs, which could consume more than 50 calories per lb bodyweight and still remain lean and fit (provided they were working).

The number of calories considered requisite to retain condition in the housedog needs to be increased in growing dogs, also during cold weather, and in pregnancy, and in lactating bitches.

In estimating the number of calories required, body surface is actually more important than weight.

In a small breed, such as a Chihuahua or Yorkshire Terrier, the basic metabolic rate is inversely proportional to that of a large dog such as a Great Dane or Pyrenean, since in dogs with a large body surface there is far greater loss of body heat.

Growing puppies require twice as many calories for each pound of their weight as adult dogs would need. Arnold and Elvelyem determined that a puppy weighing 21 oz required 282 calories, but as soon as it attained the weight of 10 lb it would require only 900 calories through an entire day.

The following list of the calories present in *one ounce* of each of a number of popular foods is shown below:

Food substance	*Calories per oz*
Beef	50–100
Mutton	70–80
Average dog biscuit (plain)	100–125
Wholemeal bread	70
White bread (not recommended)	75
Whole egg	46
Liver	40
Fresh milk	20
Oatmeal porridge (made with water)	12
,, ,, (made with milk)	15 (approx)
Tinned dog foods (about)	50–55
Lard	260
Suet	262

From the above it will be seen that a mixture of beef, 0·5 lb (say 600 calories), liver, 2 oz (80 calories), biscuit, 4 oz (400 calories) milk, 5 oz (100 calories) would supply a diet containing a total of 1,180 calories. Allowing 40 calories for each pound body weight, this would feed a 30 lb house-dog for a day and permit it to take normal exercise.

Alternatively, a diet containing an almost equal number of calories could be provided by 4 oz of tinned dog food (200 calories), 4 oz biscuit (400 calories), and 10 oz of milk (200 calories) with 4 oz wholemeal bread (280 calories.)

The above examples show how, with a knowledge of food values, the changes may be rung to provide a varied diet and, on occasion, practice economy. Due account will have to be paid to (*a*) palatability, (*b*) digestibility and (c) bulk.

12

Food Components

Briefly, these are proteins, carbohydrates, fats, water, mineral salts, and vitamins with a number of important trace elements. In addition, many foods contain a proportion of indigestible material—roughage—usually animal or vegetable fibre. This serves to dilute the food, separate its particles, and retain moisture.

Most dogs thrive better when their food contains a proportion of roughage, but in puppies and young dogs, and even in some adults, too much may give rise to bowel irritation and diarrhoea.

PROTEINS

The main source of protein used in feeding dogs is derived from flesh.

Flesh

The flesh or meat covering an animal's body is not, as many imagine, simply a body tissue designed to fill the space between bone and skin, but it actually consists of contractile muscle, the source of all bodily movements.

To put it in another way, each pound of steak represents a pound of contractile muscle. Each muscle is made up of countless bundles of muscle fibres separated, one from the other, by partitions of fibrous tissue, a variable amount of the same fibrous tissue intermingling with the muscle fibres also.

The older, or the more active, the animal, the greater is the proportion of fibrous tissue, whereas in the well fed and indolent a certain amount of fat also finds its way in and between the bundles. The relative proportions of muscle fibre, connective tissue and fat, decide whether the flesh from the carcass of a dead animal will be tough or tender.

Dogs do not chew flesh that has been cut up into moderate-sized pieces, but bolt it whole. In a state of nature, the accepted way to eat flesh is to drag it off the bones by the united force of the canine and incisor teeth and swallow it without further chewing. This is rather different from swallowing it in lumps the size of a hen's egg or larger, but it has never been shown that swallowing lumps of flesh, as large as will pass down the oesophagus, ever did a dog any harm.

Eaten in the natural way, the flesh is actually pulped, apart from odd pieces that may be torn off the carcass whole, and therefore are easily digested.

Theoretically, it is not normal for a dog to live mainly on large lumps of meat, and to overcome this many owners and also manufacturers of canned foods may resort to the mincing machine. The main difference is that dogs that bolt their food seldom digest the central part of each 'lump' swallowed, and, accordingly, a certain amount of undigested meat passes out in the faeces. In some cases this amounts to 20 per cent of the amount fed to the dog. Accordingly, some dogs will eat their own droppings or even those of other dogs, simply because they contain undigested flesh.

Those who own dogs that practise this habit should cut down the meat ration, replace it with a proportion of biscuit, and invest the savings in a mincing machine.

The term 'meat', unlike 'flesh', may include various internal organs such as heart, liver, kidney, melt (spleen), tripe, or even cow's udder.

There is little doubt that beef is the safest and most palatable of all the animal protein foods available to the dog and it suits the digestive capabilities of the majority.

Puppies will begin to lick raw, scraped beef from the attendant's fingers by the 21st day, and from then on will digest and thrive on a diet of eggs, milk, glucose, with gradually increasing amounts of scraped meat, until their sixth week.

From then on, their diet may be supplemented by the

addition of a meal made from lightly cooked wholemeal biscuit, finely ground, soaked in milk or water, and added to the egg and milk. When the proportion of meat is greater than the puppy's digestive juices can cope with, some of the undigested meat will pass out in the faeces and may be re-eaten by the puppy, or its fellows, unless the mother takes charge of the situation and gets there first. This is one reason why small puppies require 'defaecation drill' and attention to their posterior cleanliness.

The appetite for raw beef is best developed at an early age since many dogs introduced to it later in life refuse to touch it. Raw beef, chopped small or minced, is better for dogs at all ages than cooked beef provided it has been passed fit for human consumption. Uncooked meat sold at a low price may contain disease germs or parasites, and apart from being possibly dangerous for the dog, may be equally so for the person who has to handle it. Knives used for cutting up raw meat should be carefully sterilised afterwards. Anthrax, tuberculosis, salmonella infection, and a great many other diseases can be spread by an uncleaned knife that has been used for cutting up uncooked meat of dubious origin. Knacker's meat, even when 'sterilised' on the premises, should always be well boiled before feeding it to a dog.

Apart from disease and parasites present in the salvaged animal carcass, the premises and the knives and utensils may be contaminated with leptospirosis carried by rats; moreover, even when meat is cooked before sale it may be contaminated by unclean hands and knives and even by its wrappings. It is always wise to handle such meat with gloved hands and to sterilise very carefully all dishes or knives used in preparing it for consumption. Such advice may possibly be scorned by many fanciers who up to the present have been lucky, but those who have first-hand knowledge of why and how cattle reach the knacker's yard, and of the variety of animal diseases communicable to mankind, prefer to take no unnecessary risks.

The greater part of the whole animal body consists of

protein. Meat, as fed to dogs, consists of protein, fibre and a variable proportion of fat. Proteins occur in a great many forms, and a variable chemical constitution in both plants and animals, but all of them are made up of combinations of carbon, hydrogen, oxygen, nitrogen, and variable amounts of sulphur.

Within the intestine the proteins present in food are hydrolised to amino-acids, and in this form they are absorbed from the intestine into the blood of the liver. Proteins are essential to the formation of new body tissue, as well as to repairing tissue wastage. They also provide energy and are essential in maintaining health.

Proteins may be of either animal or vegetable origin. Their value depends solely upon the types of essential amino-acid each contains. So far as tissue repair and replacement is concerned, some proteins are more valuable than others since they are consumed by the body with a minimum of waste.

Generally speaking, proteins of animal origin are preferable to those of vegetable source, since the latter may lack certain of the essential amino-acids—or, if these are present, they may not be so in correct proportions. Proteins, lacking certain essentials, may be encountered in maize, while wheat gluten, soya bean meal and meals prepared from bean, peanut or sunflower seeds, may contain proteins harmful to dogs.

When a protein is digested and utilised in the body, heat is produced, together with the liberation of carbon dioxide, water, and variable quantities of nitrogenous waste products. Two of these, urea and ammonia, are excreted in sweat and urine and, to some extent, through the bowel. By chemical tests it is possible to determine the intake and output of nitrogen from the tissues, and in this way it can be determined whether or not the body is making proper use of its protein intake. This depends a great deal upon the condition of the kidneys and whether they remain healthy.

Although carbohydrates and fats provide heat and energy in a way similar to that provided by proteins, it has been proved that the inclusion in the diet of a minimum proportion of protein, whether animal or vegetable, is necessary to maintain life. In order to estimate the minimum requirement it is necessary to take into account both its amino-acid content and its degree of digestibility. The average amount of digestible protein is about 80 per cent, the remaining 20 per cent being lost through the bowel.

Making every allowance, it has been estimated that at least 15 per cent of every dog's entire ration should consist of high-grade animal protein, according to breed, size, weight, and work. As an alternative, it may contain 15 per cent of vegetable protein with the addition of 5 per cent of animal protein.

Puppies at the time of weaning, and for a few weeks after, require 18 to 25 per cent of protein, according to their breed, and this may be derived largely from milk. The next best is blood albumen, and then casein, derived from cheese.

Yeast contains 41·5 per cent of crude protein, and may be fed to puppies in powdered form with advantage from ten to twelve weeks onward after their stomachs have become accustomed to a variety of foods. Yeast is noted mainly for its vitamin B content. Care must be taken to reinforce the diet with sufficient vitamins A and D, supplied either by small doses of cod-liver or halibut-liver oil.

In spite of popular belief, it has been shown that dogs thrive perfectly on suitable vegetable proteins, so long as the essential amino-acids are present in sufficient quantity. Nevertheless, since the constitution of vegetable proteins is less easily calculable or surmised, it is still advisable to include not less than 5 to 10 per cent of meat to provide animal protein, because animal protein often carried antibodies that provide resistance against certain diseases.

Young puppies in their nest derive such antibodies from their mother's milk, and although this may increase their chances of survival up to their 7th or 8th week it may also be to the puppy's disadvantage if the presence of such antibodies is capable of destroying man-made vaccines containing an attenuated virus. Great care must be taken so that such vaccines are administered at the time when the antibodies from the milk cease to be present, or after the use of milk is discontinued.

Puppies reared entirely by hand on milk-substitutes may miss this natural source of temporary immunity. The best substitute for milk so far as antibodies are concerned is egg-yolk but where fresh blood can be obtained (as from an abattoir), allowed to clot and the serum drawn off, this when added to milk in small quantities will often allow puppies to be reared entirely without the natural milk of the bitch, with perfect results.

The next best source of animal protein for raising young puppies in the nest is prepared by soaking raw, minced beef in *lukewarm* water containing one teaspoonful of common salt to each pint.

The product is then diluted with an equal portion of fresh milk and some fresh cow's cream added, together with a sprinkling (about 2 per cent) of glucose.

Although it is not completely applicable to the subject at this stage, it may not be amiss to point out that it is imperative when feeding young puppies to slightly increase the cream content of cows' milk to approximate with that contained in the milk of the bitch, which is a good deal richer.

Growing puppies will take about 20 per cent of protein in the form of casein in their diet.

Experiments in adding amino-acids to dog foods have shown that they should never be added singly, but in combination. The addition of a single amino-acid such as lysine to a diet of wheaten flour and small quantities of meat, *partially* overcame the '*fright complex*' brought on by this type of feeding, but the complex was completely overcome when other fatty acids were administered in addition to the lysine.

Similar 'fright' symptoms may appear when commercial wheat gluten forms a part of the ration, but it is possible that this substance may possess toxic properties, apart from the unsuitability of its protein and carbohydrate content. In any case it would appear that a number of 'essential' fatty acids are required from the digestion of protein, if complete health is to be maintained.

This indicates the advantages of variety in feeding, and it is probable that it is good practice to feed alternately or together as many different kinds of animal protein as can be found possible, such as a variety of 'meats', egg, yeast, cheese and, *occasionally*, a little fish. Remember always that the addition of raw, uncleaned tripe or something resembling the content of the herbivorous stomach is what all dogs need, even if it is difficult to obtain in these hygienic times!

Experimental dogs given lysine as their fatty acid do not thrive even when additional quantities are given but regain their weight when other proteins or other fatty acids are added to the diet.

A sufficiency of proteins is essential if continuous rapid growth is to be maintained in young dogs. A deficiency of protein slows down growth so that young dogs thus deprived seldom attain the normal standard weight when they become fully developed.

A dog or any other animal is said to be in a state of *nitrogen equilibrium*, when the amount of nitrogen (an essential part of protein) taken in the food, equals the amount of nitrogen excreted through the kidneys, as the waste products urea and ammonia, in the urine.

To a lesser extent some of these are excreted in the sweat, although sweat glands are believed to exist in the dog only in the nose, lips, and feet. This may be only partly true since some body glands may discharge sweat into the hair follicles. It has been observed on many occasions that badly frightened dogs, as well as greyhounds after a fast race, exhibit a marked dampness of the skin and coat, and it may well be that there is greater surface sweating in the dog than is generally believed.

A dog can be kept alive on protein alone if this is fed in sufficient quantity to maintain nitrogen equilibrium plus an extra amount sufficient to provide energy for locomotion and various bodily requirements.

Thus, it might be possible for a dog to live on raw meat alone if it received sufficient of it. It would be necessary to administer vitamins and, if the meat was lean, it would probably be necessary to provide oil or fat also, which is not the same as feeding protein alone. This would not in any way resemble the natural food of the wild dog, which, as a rule, eats meat only after it has satisfied its carbohydrate requirements and its needs for vitamins, together with its natural intake of vegetable protein by gorging itself (so far as competition will permit) on the contents of the stomach or stomachs of its victim.

A dog of 25 lb weight (Cocker Spaniel size) fed on protein and deprived of carbohydrates and fats, would require 1,000 calories of food a day, which would be supplied by 12 to 18 oz of uncooked, lean meat, according to its quality, as well as to the ability of the dog to digest and make full use of it.

When carbohydrate and fat are included, less meat will be needed but even when the supply of the former is adequate a certain amount of protein (15 to 20 per cent) *must* be included in order to maintain nitrogen equilibrium.

Casein, the protein constituent of milk, is ideal for feeding growing puppies, either in powdered form as dried milk, or as dry, powdered cheese, which can be added to their food in quantity as high as 30 per cent. However, digestibility comes into the picture at this point, for while most dogs and puppies can digest casein with ease, not all can take a lot of cheese if it has full fat content. McKay found that about four-fifths of the protein in a mixed diet is absorbed while the remaining fifth passed out in the faeces. This is one of the reasons why some dogs eat their own, or other dog's droppings, as previously mentioned.

Among the less easily digestible foods containing vegetable proteins are some of the commercial preparations of wheat gluten, peanut meal, soya meal, and sunflower meal. The bleaching of flour by the use of agene (nitrogen trichloride), now discarded, fortunately, gives rise to hysteria (running fits) in dogs fed on this bleached product. During and before the war years 'hysteria' in dogs became rampant—a form of agene poisoning.

Dried yeast which contains 41·5 per cent of crude protein,

and a rather similar percentage of carbohydrate, is a valuable contribution to the daily menu when given in small amounts at one time, up to one ounce of yeast a day for a large dog. It also provides many, but not all, of the vitamins of the B complex.

Certain other experiments on feeding growing puppies have shown that their diet should contain not less than 17·2 per cent of protein if their growth rate is to remain steadily rising on a chart.

The feeding of 10·6 per cent of protein in company with other essential food elements, maintained health in young puppies but failed to maintain a steady rate of growth. This increased through a varying range until it reached 17·2 per cent of protein, and beyond this point no further improvement in growth rate could be perceived. Generally speaking, better results are obtained when the protein is derived from a number of sources rather than from one particular protein.

The table below shows the percentage of protein and carbo hydrates in certain foods:

Food	*Dry matter*	*Crude protein*	*Carbohydrates*
Potato	23·8	2·1	19·7
Cabbage	11·0	1·5	5·9
Maize	87·0	9·9	69·2
,, (flaked)	89·0	9·8	72·5
Bread (stale)	66·2	8·0	55·5
Soya bean meal	88·7	44·7	31·9
Whole milk	12·8	3·4	4·8
Milk whey	6·6	6·7	5·0
Whole milk (dried)	95·8	25·5	37·4
Whale meat	88·0	60·0	
Bran	87·0	14·7	52·1
Yeast (dried)	93·7	41·5	41·4
Pure meat meal	89·2	72·2	
Whole fish meal	87·0	61·0	
Ox liver	80·0	15·6 (glycogen)	3·5
Bones	variable	15.0	10–12
Kidney	80.0	13·4	
Fatty tissues		14·8	

The composition of uncooked beef depends on the quality and the proportion of fat present. A fair average of butcher's meat as fed to dogs might be: Water, 75 per cent, Protein, 18 to 20 per cent, Fat, 3 per cent, Carbohydrate, 1 per cent, Salts, 1 to 1·5 per cent.

Muscle also contains an important but variable quantity of glycogen in its substance which during life is constantly being used up for the production of energy and replaced by sugar derived from liver glycogen and from blood sugar.

During the process of digestion proteins are broken down by various *enzymes*, the most important being pepsin, which is present in the gastric juice produced by the walls of the stomach.

Another very important digestive juice is secreted by the pancreas and also by the glands of the intestinal walls. This is known as *trypsin*. It is composed of several digestive juices, some of which deal with proteins, others with carbohydrates.

CARBOHYDRATES

The carbohydrates are compounds of carbon, hydrogen and oxygen. They form an extensive group, comprising starch and its derivatives, the various forms of sugar, and cellulose, which might be likened to the connective tissue of plants and vegetables.

Glucose, which is animal starch, is present in the muscles, liver and other organs, together with minute amounts of sugar in the blood, and greater quantities (lactose) in milk.

A large amount of the carbohydrate eaten by a dog is turned into fat, or is oxidised into carbon dioxide and water during the time it is supplying heat and energy to the body.

The dog has little or no digestive enzyme (ptyalin or amylase) in its saliva, as we have, and the carbohydrates it consumes do not undergo any degree of mouth digestion. This is one reason why dogs do not chew their food in the same way that a cat does, but swallow lumps of meat and biscuit almost whole, giving one or two chops with the molar teeth merely to reduce the food to a size that enables it to pass down the oesophagus. The digestion of the food is then left to the activity of juices derived from the stomach, the pancreas, and the glands present in the lining of the small intestine.

In spite of the absence of a digestive juice in its saliva, the dog is capable of digesting and utilising large quantities of starchy foods, hydrolising the carbohydrate mainly by means of amylase derived from the pancreas. McKay has shown that dogs thrive satisfactorily when the food contains up to 50 to 60 per cent of starch and/or other carbohydrates.

Cellulose, the substance that encloses grain and forms the outer skin of most plants, is partly broken in the dog's intestine, but it is finally rendered almost completely digestible by fermentation. This fermentation does not take place so much in the intestine of the dog but in the stomach (or stomachs) of the animals the dog would normally devour in a state of nature. In the rumen (first stomach) of a deer, for example, the cellulose is broken down by fermentation into glucose and fatty acids. This liberates carbohydrates and proteins in a condition with which the digestive apparatus of the dog is fully able to deal.

As has been stated earlier in this book, this is one of the reasons why dogs and other so-called carnivorous animals derive enormous benefit from eating the stomach contents of a ruminant or smaller herbivorous animal (such as a rabbit) whenever the opportunity arises, either when the animal has been caught and killed by the individual or by the pack, or when it has been killed by a larger carnivorous animal that has eaten its fill and left a little over for the scavengers.

This is why the larger carnivora such as lions and tigers, kept in captivity, do not retain their condition and thrive as they would do in freedom, unless they are supplied not only with meat, but also with the uncleaned tripe and paunches of the animals upon which normally they would feed.

Whether the dog thrives and retains good condition and health depends largely upon its ability to secrete sufficient digestive juices of good quality from the pancreas and intestinal glands into the small intestine.

Fortunately for dogs, as well sometimes for their owners, modern science can produce pancreatic enzymes in a capsule, and food can be predigested and remain palatable. Many lives, human and otherwise, can now be prolonged indefinitely, so far as digestive deficiencies are concerned.

The pancreas is a glandular structure lying in a curve formed by the pyloric end of the stomach and the duodenum, which is the first portion of the small intestine immediately following the stomach.

The pancreas secretes not only digestive enzymes into the intestine, but also very important hormone, *insulin*, into the bloodstream.

Insulin regulates the amount of sugar present in the blood. Any excess of sugar in the circulation acts as a stimulus for the secretion of more insulin. When insufficient insulin is secreted from the pancreas—or is available—the condition known as diabetes makes its appearance.

Any defect, or abnormality of the pancreas, hereditary or acquired, may result in lack of insulin and sometimes, also, in a deficiency of pancreatic digestive juices, resulting in inability to make full use of starchy foods. This is a common cause of loss of condition in dogs and inability to put on fat in spite of heavy feeding.

The juices secreted into the small intestine by the pancreas and intestinal glands contain:

(*a*) *Trypsin*, which contains several different enzymes. This digests any proteins that have escaped their full treatment within the stomach, converting them into fatty acids which the body can absorb and use.
(*b*) *Steapsin*, mainly concerned with the digestion of fat.
(*c*) *Pancreatic amylase* (amylopsin)

Trypsin contains also an enzyme, *ptyalin*, which is present in the saliva of many animals, but is absent in that of the dog. It hydrolises starch and converts it into dextrins and maltose.

In addition, the pancreas secretes, in company with the digestive glands in the stomach wall, an enzyme, *rennin*, which coagulates milk. Rennin is present in considerable quantities in the digestive juices of all young mammals, including puppies, and in less quantity in adults. Curdling of the milk retards its passage through the intestine and helps its digestion.

Although milk contains proteins, mainly *casein*, practically the only carbohydrate present in milk is milk sugar (lactose). The amount of sugar in cow's milk is 4·8 per cent.

Although carbohydrates do not comprise any considerable part of the living animal, those taken in the food are converted by the action both of enzymes and bacteria, normally present in the intestine, into sugars (monosaccharides) and simple fatty acids, and in these forms they are absorbed into the body.

In most animals the breakdown of carbohydrates in the course of digestion begins in the mouth though, as has been stated earlier, this does not apply to the dog.

Like other carnivorous animals, the dog may convert a portion of the carbohydrates it consumes into fats, so that the total body fat may be considerably in excess of the amount of fat eaten, and more than can be accounted for by the transformation of some of the fat eaten by the dog, into body fat. This comes about through certain amino-acids derived from proteins being converted into sugar within the body and the subsequent conversion of this sugar into fat.

But, on the whole, nearly all the protein consumed by a *normal* dog is burnt up to provide energy, and the main source of body fat is carbohydrate plus any excess of fat fed to it. But all dogs, like all men, are not normal, and it is possible for a dog to become too fat on a diet almost wholly protein, even when protein is employed for the purpose of reducing its weight.

Normal, healthy dogs with a natural supply of pancreatic juice are well able to digest cooked starch, as present in biscuits, with the output of a useful number of calories.

Experimentally, dogs have been maintained in good condition on diets containing 66 per cent of cane sugar (sucrose). Many attempts have been made to add molasses to dog biscuits but, curiously perhaps, very few dogs will persist in eating sweetened foods, however keenly they may accept them on the first few occasions.

A mistaken idea exists that dogs fed largely on carbohydrates develop skin disorders, but this need not be the case provided they are not deprived of essential vitamins. Many animals that live completely on a carbohydrate diet—the ruminants for example—synthesise most of their own vitamins, particularly those of the B-complex, within their own stomachs, and it is possible that dogs might be able to produce at least some of their own vitamins if their stomachs and intestines contained more vegetable and carbohydrate content than meat.

This is not an attempt to extol the virtues of carbohydrate feeding for dogs, but simply to point out that when carbohydrates are fed largely or exclusively to dogs, it is essential that vitamins of the B-complex should be added to their diet and, possibly, vitamins A and D in the form of cod-liver oil or halibut-liver oil. This is probably the reason for the popularity of yeast products, which are the most prolific source of vitamin B.

One disadvantage of feeding carbohydrates is that, unless exercise can be unlimited, carbohydrates sufficient to provide energy may result also in the laying down of surplus fat.

FATS

Normal dogs require not less than 5 per cent of fat in their diet if they are to remain comfortably plump, and carry good coats. As much as 10 per cent can be fed, temporarily, to a dog that has lived on a fat-deficient diet, or half-starved, without causing digestive upsets, except perhaps in a few individual cases in which there is fat-sensitivity—the so-called chronically 'gastric' case, to use a common expression.

Every dog, however, appears to have its own special fat

requirement; while some appear to be unable to digest mutton fat, and others pork fat (lard), they thrive on a fairly high proportion of beef fat added to their regular diet. In the absence of a fat ration, the dog uses up fat already stored in its body, until the fat content of the whole body falls to 6 per cent, after which emaciation becomes observable.

It is being able to maintain the balance between the laying down of fat and its regular rate of absorption that spells success—not a particularly easy thing to do in these days of building congestion and motor traffic, which limit the possibility of either man or dog taking sufficient exercise.

The type of fat within the body depends in large measure upon the diet. If it comes from the food in the form of butter, beef fat, cream or lard, the dog's fat remains soft and the dog appears unduly obese.

If, however, the source of the fat is digested carbohydrate, the fat in the body is much harder, and it is possible for the dog to carry a considerable quantity of such fat, firmly moulded into or around the body, with the dog looking fairly normal, certainly not obese.

Although both fat and carbohydrate foods provide energy, they play quite different parts in the metabolism of the body, and the one cannot be subsituted for the other, both fat and carbohydrate being necessarily present in the same diet.

The inclusion of sufficient fat in the diet appears to have a definite value in maintaining bitch fertility but at no time should the proportion of fat fed to brood bitches exceed 5 per cent of the total ration. This applies also to lactating bitches during the summer, though rather more can be fed to them when the weather and the accommodation are cold.

Fat is very necessary in connection with the nourishment and well-being of the skin, and in this connection one must include the ears, which are lined with skin even down the ear canal. It has been proved that a number of skin diseases, including a fair proportion of cases of so-called chronic 'ear-canker',[1] respond to treatment consisting of feeding fat, or unsalted bacon in the feed daily, while the benefit derived from quite small amounts of pure, fresh linseed oil (*not* boiled oil) is well known to many breeders.

A shortage of fat in the diet may give rise in some dogs, principally the long-eared varieties, to a purulent form of ear canker.

Excess of fat fed to dogs lessens the appetite for other necessary foods and, even if it fails to excite biliousness and vomiting, it may retard growth in young animals.

Young dogs and recently weaned puppies are far less able than older animals to digest either meat proteins or fats. Rancid fats such as stale lard and rancid cod-liver oil, are capable of destroying vitamins A and E in the body. One useful effect of a store of fat within the body is that it may help to combat certain types of infection, especially those attacking the skin.

DIET AND DEVELOPMENT

Stockyard (Philadelphia), 1941, kept animals under carefully controlled conditions of diet, taking care to reduce variations due to environmental conditions to a minimum.

He showed that apart from genetic differences between light and heavy bone, the quality of bone can be influenced a great deal by the diet and the amount and nature of the exercise given to the growing puppy. He demonstrated that heavy bone may be the product of heavy feeding, probably with restricted exercise. He found that only a part of the changes during growth were the effect of breed but that puppies from some of the more newly established breeds were more influenced so far as their development went by varying types of environment than puppies of old-standing breeds.

High feeding during the first three or four months tends to produce heavy bone, a long back, large feet, and relatively

[1] It must be remembered that many cases of persistent canker are due to the presence of 'grass seeds'.

short legs and neck. He compared the changes in puppies thus treated with similar changes in early-maturing sheep as described by Hammond (1932) in this country.

Riser (1963) (*J. Small Aml. Practice*) discussing hip dysplasia in the dog, stated that high feeding favours its development, while other observers have stated that this condition can often be combated by keeping puppies in cages for the first few months of their life. That the onset of the condition may be retarded in this way may be likely but whether its development can be avoided completely is open to doubt. Many dogs that show no actual distress and no very obvious lameness may be shown on X-ray examination to be affected.

Burns and Fraser in *Genetics of the Dog* point out that moderate feeding up to five or six months old followed by a period of high nutrition tend to thicken the long bones of the legs and to coarsen the skull. They state that in a breed such as the English Cocker Spaniel, which should possess short backs, heavy bone, and fine long skulls, the growth period of each part has to be watched and the diet nicely adjusted to develop these mutually antagonistic show points.

Too much exercise may cause the legs of Bulldogs to grow long, while rickets can produce the kind of limbs seen in achondroplastic breeds (having shortened limbs dependent on disturbances in the ossification of the cartilages of long bones).

13

Vitamins

Vitamins are a group of organic substances with a known chemical formula. Although they may be required only in small, or minute amounts, they are essential not only to the well-being of the dog but also to its existence. The absence of certain vitamins in the diet gives rise to specific deficiency diseases that are well recognised.

Some animals, notably the herbivora, are able to synthesise a great many, but not all, of the necessary vitamins during the fermentation of food in their stomachs and intestines. The carnivorous animals, including the dog, with the exception of the Basenji, the Hairless Dogs, and occasional individuals in other breeds, seldom devour enough fresh vegetable material to supply their vitamin needs, but they make up for it by gutting the animals they kill and devouring their stomach and bowel contents, usually long before they start on the flesh.

Dogs in domestication, deprived of this natural source of vitamins, have to depend upon the vitamins present in, or added to, their artificial diets. They may obtain some of their requirements from fats and meat, from wheatmeal used in making biscuits, and also from cod-liver oil and yeast products, or from specially fermented food supplements, which may contain rare vitamins unlikely to be obtained from any source other than stomach contents or the artificial supplement.

It is probable that a number of vitamins, mostly water-soluble, have not yet been identified and it is because they are produced in the fermenting contents of the herbivorous stomachs that the value of paunch contents is so great, especially among the carnivorous zoo animals which often fail to thrive in a cage unless provided with their natural food, including paunch contents at regular intervals.

Different dogs belonging to different breeds vary in their vitamin requirements as regards their variety, quantity and source, and among animals, generally, this specialisation becomes very apparent. For example, vitamin C (ascorbic acid) needs to be added to the food of certain species, frequently including human beings; but dogs do not require this addition because they are able to manufacture their own vitamin C in their intestines. Some domesticated dogs will eat grapes, oranges, and other fruit, and foxes, when they lost their rabbits and rabbit guts, took to eating fruit and vegetables.

So can herbivorous animals with large stomachs, full of fermenting food, synthesise their own vitamin B-complex, probably in greater variety than it can be purchased from a chemist's shop. Dogs, especially those fed mainly on a diet of flesh, cannot do this, although it is possible they might do so if it was supplemented by vegetable material and carbohydrates.

Under natural conditions, and quite commonly in rural areas, dogs, together with other carnivorous animals such as foxes, habitually eat dry cowdung, given the opportunity, and in this way increase their intake of vitamin B.

All kinds of animals need vitamins A and D since they are associated with growth and with development of the embryo, as well as being essential to the normal growth of the bony skeleton.

In nature, vitamin A is found in the oily content of the livers of fishes, in egg yolk, mammalian liver, milk, cream and butter, and in the flesh and fat of animals. Kidney and liver are rich in this vitamin but very little is to be found in lean meat.

It is not present in plants, especially green vegetables in its completed form, but a great many plants and roots, especially cabbage and carrots, contain substances known as *carotenes,* which are yellow, or otherwise pigmented materials known as *provitamins* because they become converted into vitamin A when they are taken into the body.

The carotene can be stored in the liver of the animal which

eats it, until required by the body. In the nursing female the carotene may not be completely converted into vitamin but can be excreted in the milk in some individuals as carotene instead of vitamin A. This is what gives the yellow colour to the milk of Jersey cows, and when such milk is swallowed by the puppy it becomes converted into the vitamin.

Vitamin A in milk, as well as carotene in green food, are rapidly oxidised by sunlight and storage, especially if the foodstuff also contains iron as a mineral supplement.

Dog biscuits and meal, fortified by cod-liver oil, must soon lose their vitamin A content unless the goods are specially packed. It is also well known that an excessive dosage with cod-liver oil or the addition of the oil to packaged food, will destroy the vitamin E content entering the animal's body, and this is particularly the case when the cod-liver oil is stale and rancid.

Vitamin E is particularly associated with fertility and infertility and it is believed by many breeders that a deficiency is the cause of much of the failure of bitches to breed, or to carry litters to their full term. It is possible that the destruction of vitamin E by an excess of cod-liver oil or by feeding foods containing the oil, may have this effect, presuming that vitamin E is in reality the fertility vitamin, as it is said to be.

Puppies lacking vitamin A fail to grow, and finally die, while a deficiency of this vitamin in the diet of the pregnant bitch, especially during the first four weeks of gestation, may cause abortion, malformation of puppies, or the birth of dead puppies.

Night blindness (not in this instance to be confused with progressive retinal atrophy) can be produced in young puppies soon after the eyes have opened when the dam is deliberately kept short of vitamin A. If the deficiency is maintained in the puppies, convulsions and kidney disorders may follow.

Another common condition in puppies arising from lack of this vitamin is soreness of the eyes and surrounding eyelids, a condition that is very common in puppies when the bitch has been deprived of a sufficiency of vitamin A during early pregnancy.

In other cases there may be a reduction in tear secretion so that the normally clear, glassy surface of the cornea becomes dry and slightly cracked, with ensuing ulceration.

In young dogs, vitamin A encourages growth and helps to keep the skin supple and the coat glossy. To some extent this vitamin is beneficial in warding off certain puppy infections. A lack of the vitamin may give rise to deafness,

Unlike farm animals, puppies come into the world without a great deal of vitamin A stored in the liver, mainly because, unlike the former, bitches do not eat grass and cabbage containing carotene. It is imperative that the puppy should receive a plentiful supply from early in its lifetime. This is best done by feeding eggs, or cod-liver or halibut-liver oil to the in-whelp bitch and the nursing mother, who will pass it on to the puppies in her milk. One must be careful to continue the vitamin during weaning, which is the dangerous time when a shortage may otherwise occur.

The vitamin A requirement of the dog appears to be somewhat variable according to size and, of course, the particular breed. Udal recommended 100 international units (I.U.) of vitamin A a day for every kilogram (about 2 lb) of bodyweight in order to ensure a reserve of the vitamin within the liver. Growing puppies require a minimum of 60 I.U. per kilogram of bodyweight daily.

A dog of, say, 25 lb weight, would require about 1,250 I.U. derived from a good quality cod-liver oil, the vitamin content of which should be shown on the label. This would be in the region of about 2 teaspoonsful of oil, though the quantity must necessarily depend upon the nature of the diet consumed.

There is an element of danger in overdosing since, as has already been mentioned, excess of vitamin A may counteract the effect of vitamin E present in the food, but as there is usually an abundance of vitamin E in the normal diet of the dog, the risk is not so great as might appear. A lot of the vitamin E is obtained from whole wheat flour incorporated in biscuit.

VITAMIN D

This is known as the anti-rachitic vitamin, the one that helps to keep bones straight and healthy, and prevents rickets. It occurs mainly as Vitamin D3 in the oil extracted from fish livers.

There is no D1 recognised, but vitamin D2 is produced by the action of sunlight on a substance named cholesterol, which is present in skin. It can also be formed when light falls on certain foodstuffs, including vegetable material, which subsequently may be fed to a dog.

This applies to grass clippings that have partly dried in the sun and appear to have an attraction for dogs, many of which devour them greedily when the opportunity arises.

Vitamins D2 and D3 are somewhat unstable and are apt to disappear from packed dog foods after a short period of storage.

Rickets

Since rickets is one of the manifestations of a deficiency of vitamin D, it is perhaps a fitting time to discuss its causation and, so far as possible, its treatment, mainly preventative.

Vitamin D plays an important part in the assimilation of calcium and phosphorous from the intestine and their transfer to and from the body and the bones. Although Vitamin D exerts a degree of control over phosphorus and calcium balance within the body, it cannot operate successfully when the relative proportion of these two substances is grossly disturbed. In growing puppies the intake of each—the Ca:P ratio—should be 1·2:1.

When the calcium is in excess of the phosphorus to the extent of 2:1, the calcification of bone in dogs under 18 months is greatly impaired. It is possible, however, that in such cases the administration of vitamins D2 or D3 may exert a moderate degree of control.

The fact remains, however, that *calciferol*, as the commonly used form of the vitamin is termed, is not specific against the development of rickets unless the Ca: P balance is kept at the correct level.

An excess of calcium in a puppy's diet may be more harmful than a deficiency, and the custom of feeding more and more calcium to a rickety puppy is far more likely to do harm than good.

The minimum amount of vitamin D2 necessary to avoid rickets when the diet is correctly adjusted, is approximately 20 I.U. per kilogram of bodyweight daily. A kilogram is roughly about 2 lb.

Pure cod-liver oil contains about 6,000 I.U. of vitamin D in each fluid ounce of oil.

It seems likely that, apart from dietary discrepancies, a tendency to rickets may have a hereditary background, and in certain strains and circumstances the condition may appear when puppies are correctly fed and exercised and kept in suitable environment. Sometimes these cases become so exaggerated that the puppy cannot stand at all on its forelimbs and nothing appears to be in any sense a remedy.

Osteogenesis imperfecta is a bone disease not infrequently seen in the larger breeds, particularly in greyhounds. It occurs also in children. The usual history is that some puppies are born dead, some die immediately after birth, and among the survivors the majority sustain fractures of the ribs or limb bones whenever the puppies are handled or picked up and when they attempt to play with one another. The fractures appear to be practically painless, and frequently the cripples appear to be unaware of their injuries.

Survivors, after careful splinting and administration of cod-liver oil with their food, appear eventually to recover but the healed bones are usually distorted.

About forty-five years ago, this condition—obviously

hereditary—completely wiped out in South-West England one of the best-known strains of exhibition Greyhounds in the days when this breed was at its zenith. All experiments concerned with feeding the bitches with additional vitamins D2 and A during early pregnancy and the lactation period proved unsuccessful.

Avitaminosis and skin disease

Young dogs kept short of vitamin D, especially when the deficiency corresponds with lack of fat in the diet, become thin or emaciated and show a peeling off of the outer layers of the skin (epidermis). Patches of skin become more or less devoid of hair and a baldness appears in the skin surrounding the eyelids. Advanced cases of avitaminosis may develop a fatal pneumonia.

A deficiency of fat in the diet may cause a corresponding lack of cholesterol in the skin. This is the substance converted by the action of sunlight into vitamin D2. This absence or deficiency of fat can cause skin abnormalities of dogs in any breed or age.

Affected puppies are unable to produce sufficient vitamin D2, but given fat, and exercise in daylight or sunshine, they will again manufacture their own vitamin D, make good recoveries, and their skins will again become normal.

THE VITAMIN B–COMPLEX

While vitamins A and D are regarded as fat-soluble and present in animal oils, particularly in the livers of fish and other animals, in egg yolk, cream and grain, the vitamins of B-complex are regarded as being water-soluble.

Vitamin C (ascorbic acid) is also water-soluble, and it is quite likely that other water-soluble vitamins exist, as yet unscheduled. Some of these may be produced in the fermentation of vegetable material in the stomachs and intestines, particularly in those of ruminants, and it is possible that if dogs were given more vegetable food, they, too, might synthesise vitamins they now get only from the actual stomach contents of a dead herbivore, or from one of the synthetic substitutes on sale.

It should not be forgotten that the dog is still basically a wild animal that has adapted itself by a process of selection to living and feeding in an abnormal environment. When fond owners see their dogs eating certain kinds of refuse or quietly feeding in the country on dry cowdung, they are horrified and feel compelled to chastise their pets, little realising that at long last the pet has just discovered something it has lacked but unconsciously craved for throughout its lifetime.

Even in the young calf, before its first stomach—the rumen—has finally developed, it becomes necessary sometimes to administer a bolus of the stomach contents of a recently slaughtered bovine animal to provide essential vitamins and the kind of bacteria that will give rise to the type of fermentation necessary to produce more vitamin.

This increased need for B-complex vitamins is marked at weaning time when the puppy loses the vitamins supplied in its mother's milk. It then needs the whole milk, egg and cream which contains these, otherwise it will suffer a temporary check and failure to resist disease.

14

The Growing Puppy

There are many features that cannot be properly assessed during the early months of a puppy's life but which assume considerable importance by the time it has reached six months or nine months of age. First and possibly foremost among these comes the matter of the puppy's mouth.

JAWS AND TEETH

Some breeders, usually the more experienced, watch mouths constantly throughout growth, but some of the less experienced are apt to pay attention to the more visible features and imagine perhaps that they have bred a 'flier' until someone points out that the puppy lacks the scissor bite (where it is required) or is slightly overshot, or perhaps very much undershot (where it is *not* required).

What is less often observed, but is nowadays almost equally as important to the exhibitor, is the number of teeth present and the way they are placed in the gums. (Fig. 10.)

So far as jaw length is concerned and as a guide to whether the incisor teeth will end up with the correct relationship between the upper and lower sets, it should be borne in mind that the lower jaw goes on growing for a short period after growth of the upper jaw has ceased.

In other words a *slightly* overshot mouth at three months of age may be corrected by the time the puppy is eight or nine months old, but a *slightly* undershot mouth at four months is not likely to improve and may be worse at eight months. These remarks apply only to the long-headed breeds and not to the short-faced (brachycephalic) breeds in which the tendency towards an undershot mouth is greater.

A difficulty arises in a breed such as the Shih-Tzu, in

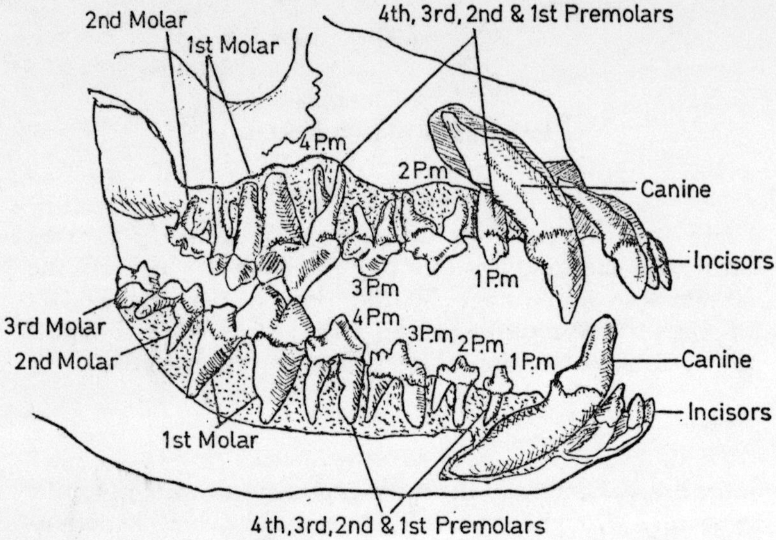

Figure 10 Dentition of the dog

which permissively there may be a slightly undershot jaw, but not to an extent where the lower incisors become visible when the lips are closed normally.

The majority of cases of undershot jaw may be regarded as incompletely recessive. In crossbreeds, where one parent is long-headed and the other short-headed (brachycephalic), the majority of the offspring are not undershot, but if these are mated again to a brachycephalic partner the puppies will be about 50 per cent undershot.

A similar incidence is seen when, for example, an undershot Terrier is mated with one with normal jaw length. Only a small proportion of the puppies may be undershot, but if the level-mouthed puppies are mated to an even slightly undershot partner, or to a carrier, at least half of the offspring will be undershot. This finding applies also in breeds that have been produced by crossing the two types, the dolichocephalic (long-headed) breeds with the brachycephalic (short-headed).

In an overshot jaw the incisor teeth may be smaller than normal and not infrequently they may fit loosely into their sockets (alveoli) so that they may be moved slightly by finger pressure.

In some breeds, strains exist in which excessively overshot jaws occur, or in which the lower jaw fails to reach its normal length. Cases of this kind are seen occasionally in Dachshunds and in various Terriers, but as such puppies may have difficulty in sucking it is unlikely that many reach maturity.

The number of teeth present is important in dogs intended for exhibition even if it has no practical bearing on the welfare of specimens intended as pets. It is a fact that the skulls of prehistoric dogs in existence show a complete absence of the first three premolar teeth, and in our modern dogs it is by no means uncommon for only two out of the normal four premolars of each upper jaw to be present.

A dog should possess three premolar teeth lying in the space between the large canine tooth of either side of the upper jaw and the fourth premolar, which is almost always present and is the largest of all the cheek teeth. This tooth operates in unison with the first molar tooth of the lower jaw, which matches it in size and shape. This fourth premolar in the upper jaw is known as the 'carnassial tooth'.

Here is a summary of the dentition of the normal dog and the changes relevant to age. The specimen under consideration might be an Alsatian or a Greyhound, but other types, such as a Poodle, must for exhibition purposes conform to the following standard of dentition.

The dog has 28 temporary teeth and either 42 or 44 permanent teeth. The puppy is born toothless.

The *temporary* canine teeth (tusks) appear at 3 to 4 weeks, and all 6 incisor teeth are present by the 4th or 5th week.

The *permanent* central and lateral incisors appear at 4 months.

The corner (end) incisors are changed at 4½ to 5 months.

Although the teeth in the upper and lower jaws are not

numerically equal, the dog has in all 22 incisors, 4 canines, 16 premolars, and 10 molars.

The permanent dental formula is (or should be) on either side of the mouth.

	Incisors	*Tusks*	*Premolars*	*Molars*
Upper jaw	3	1	4	2
Lower jaw	3	1	4	3

The largest cheek tooth in the upper jaw is the 4th premolar, and in the lower jaw, the 1st molar.

The upper jaw behind the 4 premolars carries only 2 molars, while the lower jaw carries 3 molars.

The 1st, 2nd and 3rd premolars appear at about 3 to 4 weeks and are changed for permanent premolars at between 5 and 6 months.

At about the same time, the 1st molar (the 5th cheek tooth) appears in the upper jaw. The 2nd molar (6th cheek tooth) arrives in the lower jaw at 6 to 8 months but it may be missing from the upper jaw, so that this jaw then carries only 4 premolars and 1 molar.

The possession of the 3rd molar in the bottom jaw shows that the puppy is 6 months of age or over, and that, in this country, it is due for a licence.

Irregular arrangement of the existing teeth, particularly of the incisors, is more common in Toy breeds and especially nowadays in Toy Poodles and in a less proportion of miniatures, possibly because this breed is now so popular.

The reason appears to be the growing tendency towards increased length of foreface which results in a marked diminution in the width of the end portion of the jaws in which the incisors are embedded. The alveoli, the bony sockets in which the incisors have their roots, are absent in some cases or, if present, they may not lie in a straight line and for sheer lack of room the incisor teeth overlap to the extent that they may form a double row, usually containing the original six teeth, though in rare cases there may be eight or nine, much smaller than normal, and imperfectly embedded in an alveolus and, therefore, somewhat loose and even, on occasion, held in position simply by the fleshy part of the gum.

On the other hand, some of the short-faced breeds, such as the Bulldog, and intermediate breeds, such as the Boxer, may carry supernumerary alveoli and seven incisor teeth in a row instead of the usual six.

From personal observation of Bulldogs with wide flat upper jaws, it would appear that approximately 25 per cent have seven upper incisors, although Aitchison in the *Veterinary Record* (1964, *75*, 153-4) regarded the incidence in seventy-one dogs he examined as being as high as 39 per cent.

Similarly, he found that in adult dogs the incidence of seven upper incisors was in Pekingese 1·3 per cent, Pugs 4 per cent, Boxers 26 per cent, Bullmastiffs 8 per cent, while twenty-three Mastiffs all had the normal number of six incisor teeth. In Boxers it seems difficult to get the wide muzzle required nowadays without the presence of an additional incisor.

Boxers that carry an extra incisor occasionally develop an abnormal calcification of some of the limb bones, and a number of cases have been observed by us in which enlargement of the lower end of one radius has developed, frequently associated with bone cyst, severe lameness, and pain. The condition has never, so far, responded to treatment.

EARS

Many a good dog is spoilt for exhibition on account of imperfect ears. Since ears may vary so much in size and shape, it is surprising that a type of ear has become more or less fixed for each particular breed. Generally speaking, size of ear is related to the amount of slack, loose skin carried by the dog. Many modern breeds have been bred down in size from larger progenitors, and in some of the existing breeds the skin surface has not been reduced in a degree to correspond with the reduction in body size. Common methods of using up excess of skin is to convert it into large ear flaps, skin wrinkling and dewlaps. The ear flaps of the Cocker Spaniel and the wrinkling of the face of the Bloodhound and Basset Hound are examples of attempts to overcome abnormal skin slackness. The reverse holds good in a breed such as the Black and Tan Terrier, which has a tight skin and erect ears, thin in their substance.

Alsatians often have good erect ears or dubious, 'floppy' ears, according to whether or not there is an increased thickness of the skin.

In Corgis, poor upright shoulders, combined with a short neck, may give rise to looseness of skin in the neck with a corresponding lack of ear support, so that one or both ears may droop.

Thick skin produces heavy ears which the ear muscles are unable to support in the fully erect position.

Apart from the importance of ear carriage in show dogs, those who breed and employ dogs for work frequently believe that ear carriage and the thickness and weight of the skin covering the ear cartilages has a bearing upon performance. They regard thin ears as being related to power of scent. Genetically, the size of ears and ear carriage may be influenced by two factors: firstly by skin weight (usually related to skin slackness), and secondly, by the degree of development of the muscles lying between the ear cartilage and the skin covering it.

Since in no other species does one encounter so many dissimilar types of ear, it is not surprising that dogs suffer from a variety of troubles, the majority of which are classed by the laymen under the unscientific term 'canker'. So far as treatment goes, a common diagnosis and shotgun therapy gets one nowhere.

Before considering why ears and ear canals become sore and infected, and why ears are such a universal seat of canine suffering, let us take a look at the ear and its structure.

The external ear, known as the 'ear flap' and leather, takes a number of varying shapes and sizes according to breed, or in nondescript types to their parentage, and many of these may predispose to ear infections. For example, in the Cocker Spaniel, Basset Hounds and the Poodle family, to mention only a few, the ear flaps are large, flat, and pendulous, completely sealing off the orifice of the ear canal, reducing its ventilation and interfering with the discharge of moist wax, debris, and waste material from its depths.

In many other breeds such as the Alsatian, Scottish Terrier and Collie, the ears are erect and open to the outer air, with freedom to rid themselves of waste material without hindrance.

In some other breeds the ear may be an even more complicated structure especially when the 'rose' or 'button' types, for in these the ear cartilage is bent and crinkled and, not infrequently, the inner surface of the ear and ear canal may become exposed to cold, and to external injury, often from the dog's own feet.

The external ear flap may be regarded as a sheet of cartilage, more or less flattened in those breeds possessing drooping ears, but trumpet-shaped, convoluted or creased in many other breeds. In every case the cartilage is lined internally and covered externally by skin. That of the outer surface usually carries hair, sometimes smooth and short, at others long and profuse. Normally, the inner surface carries very little hair but, on occasion, instead of its being confined to the inner edges it extends along the whole of the underlying ear surface and may even extend some way down the inner lining of the ear canal.

This is particularly so in Poodles, especially black Poodles, Bedlingtons, and Sealyhams. The hair is cast in the usual way and accumulates in the depths of the ear canal as a wet, putrefying mass, which gives rise to marked irritation.

The ear canal, which extends from the inner surface of the earflap down as far as the 'tympanum' or ear-drum, is not a simple straight tube.

Its upper orifice is moulded into shape by a peculiar kinking of the cartilage at the entrance to the canal. After this, it travels downwards as a tube, with a smooth interior of skin (not mucous membrane as in the nose). When the tube approaches its full depth, about half an inch from it, it suddenly takes a right-angled turn directed inwards towards the lower part of the skull containing the auditory mechanism (tympanum, middle and inner ears) which convey messages to the nerves leading to the brain.

This final portion of the ear canal, about half an inch or more in length, lies quite horizontally, is entirely out of sight, and cannot be completely viewed, even with the help of an electric auriscope.

The smooth skin lining the ear flap as well as the ear canal contains a number of sebaceous glands that secrete a material not unlike lanoline in consistency. This helps to keep the skin and ear duct smooth and moist. Farther down in the ear, some of these glands secrete a modified form of this sebaceous material, usually referred to as 'ear wax'. This is at first quite soft and fluid. If retained in the ear canal it may become hard and act as a foreign body.

The ear canal itself is subject to various alterations in shape as opposed to the normal. In many instances these changes appear to be hereditary. In some breeds, notably Poodles, and more recently in Labradors, the ear canal from its actual orifice downward may be no larger in diameter than a goose quill, whereas in a normal ear a veterinary surgeon should be able to introduce a pledget of cotton wool held in suitable forceps in order to clean out the whole of the upper portion of the canal.

Sometimes, only one of the two ear canals is affected, one being constricted and the other of normal size.

The portion of the ear that lies, at depth, horizontally between the termination of the perpendicular portion and the surface of the ear drum, is the part responsible, in so many instances, for the failure of simple treatments to bring any permanent relief.

Parasites, usually ear mites, find shelter in this protected space and stay well out of reach of the usual ointments and dressings. They may be reached only by irrigation of the ear carried out by skilled hands, and by fluid dressings introduced under a moderate degree of pressure. In many of the patients that grow hair far down into the ear canal there is often a firm mass of sodden material acting as a plug, preventing dressings reaching the parasites and causing deafness by pressure upon the ear drum. If a number of parasites are present, their black excrement fills the canal, and acts as an irritant, particularly in individuals sensitive to its action.

Some dogs, less sensitive, or non-allergic, go through life with caked, dirty ears, showing few signs, other than deafness. Such dogs act as carriers and can transfer eggs and mites to dogs possessing healthy ears.

Parasites may sometimes be visible against this black excrement and even seen to move by the naked eye, but in any case, the examination of a particle of the material spread on a glass slide under the low power lens of a microscope will reveal parasites when present.

At one time it was considered that ear mites were responsible, directly or indirectly, for 75 per cent of all ear cases. Although they are still of major importance, now that so many more owners are becoming 'mite-conscious', more effort is being made to keep ears clear of parasites.

Today, many cases of ear disease are due to hereditary abnormality of the ear duct and also to the tendency to grow hair right down into the deeper part of the ear lining. These are genetic features to which, so far, surprisingly little attention has been paid.

The invisible section of the ear canal is not infrequently a harbouring place for the awn of the wild barley grass which may find itself under the ear flap in autumn and travel down the ear canal until it is out of view. This happens far more often than is ever suspected and quite a number of the persistent cases of so-called 'canker' are treated with powders, lotions, and ointments by their unsuspecting owners, until one or more awns puncture the tympanum, enter the inner ear, causing abscess formation, deafness and not infrequently meningitis associated with convulsions.

Let us now enumerate some of the more common ear conditions we encounter in our dogs and see if we can pinpoint their cause, then decide how best they may be dealt with.

Just one word of warning. The recognised treatments include the insertion into the ears of insoluble powders which gravitate into the lower part of the ear canal and stay there, adding a little more rubbish to that already present. Also, when ears are 'cleaned' by their owners, they are apt to use cotton wool, tweezers, matchsticks, hairpins, the broken off segments of knitting needles, and a variety of other dangerous implements. None of these get dirt *up* out of the ear and there is a considerable risk of pushing solid waxy material and even foreign bodies such as barley awns and grass seeds farther down into the ear canal, with the result that treatment does far more harm than good.

The old idea that the inside of a dog's ear should never be wetted is pure rubbish, for pure soap and warm water is just as efficacious inside an ear as on the surface of the body. The lining of the ear canal is only skin after all, and not mucous membrane such as lines most other channels.

Syringing an ear or allowing warm fluid to gravitate into it through a soft tube is far safer than poking solid objects into an already inflamed passage, and far more effective. One may also introduce lukewarm olive oil with safety. Refrain not only from using insoluble powders but also from inserting thick, semi-solid ointments.

Nowadays, after a preliminary examination to determine, with the use of a special lamp known as an auriscope, that no foreign bodies are present in the ear canal, the veterinary surgeon will wash out the ear with a suitable antiseptic shampoo and then supply a combination of antibiotic and a corticosteroid which will do much to cleanse the ear and relieve the irritation and pain.

It is quite certain that the majority of ear cases respond to professional treatment, and in those few instances when it is impossible to reach the trouble through the ear canal, a surgical operation known as ear resection will open the passage right down to the ear drum. The end result is usually completely successful and no visible disfigurement remains.

Deafness

In young dogs, bilateral deafness may be a congenital defect more common in some breeds than others. White Bull Terriers and merle Collies are among these, but of late years deafness has appeared in other breeds and great care may have to be taken to avoid the defect becoming perpetuated.

In old dogs that have had normal hearing in earlier life, the deafness may sometimes result from a normal wearing-out process, but in some instances cleaning out the ears and removing accumulated wax and debris may effect an improvement. Quite frequently the lining of the ear duct becomes thickened, and after the ear canal has been cleaned the daily insertion of a little warm olive oil into the ear may reduce this and at least partially restore the power of hearing. In other cases the ear canal may become filled with quite large warty growths, which may require surgical removal.

More about ear mites

Quite a large proportion of puppies in the nest carry ear mites they have acquired from their dam. This indicates that, in addition to worming the bitch before mating and halfway through her pregnancy, her ears should also be cleaned and dressed with a parasiticide.

Many bitches, and dogs, carry a quantity of ear mites without showing any visible signs unless the ears are thoroughly examined and their waxy material submitted to microscopical examination. Another dog, sensitive to mites and their excretions, may pick up some of the parasites from a 'carrier' dog and exhibit great irritation within the ear canals, a 'drunken' type of action with some loss of balance which may be followed by fits.

Modern dressings are quite capable of destroying living mites provided they can make contact with them, but they do not always destroy the eggs of the parasites, which may hatch out and in a short time begin to lay more eggs.

Since affected dogs shake their heads a great deal they may throw mites and eggs onto their bedding, or they may find other cover and eventually make contact with healthy dogs.

Although most mites have their own special hosts, there is evidence that the household cat may act as a carrier and convey infection to the family dog. It is important therefore to treat both dogs and cats at the same time.

It might be as well to repeat the advice regarding the detection of barley-grass awns. The dog carrying one or more of these shows considerable distress, and usually tilts its head to one side.

The attack usually appears suddenly, usually after being in a neglected garden or a trip into the country.

Nowadays improvements in auriscopes and special forceps render it easier for the veterinary surgeon to effect removal of the awns. This is quite impossible for the owner to do for himself and even a few hours' neglect may have serious results.

15

Some Common Ailments

Two conditions seen in puppies that may be discussed briefly are vomiting and fits.

VOMITING

Vomiting—known also as emesis and vomition—must be regarded merely as a symptom, not a disease. The important thing is to determine the cause before deciding upon its importance and the line of treatment advisable.

The dog is somewhat unique in being able with little effort to throw up the contents of its stomach whenever they are unacceptable, possibly with the aid of a very slight stimulus, such as might be provided by swallowing a few blades of rough grass. Some of the birds are able to vomit with ease but rats, by some dispensation of Providence, once having eaten are quite unable to rid themselves of it by this means.

To be able to vomit, the soft palate at the hinder end of the animals' mouth must be capable of covering and closing the opening into the larynx (upper end of the windpipe), thus leaving a clear passage from the stomach to the mouth. The dog can fulfil these requirements and is, therefore, able to vomit safely with little risk of food being sucked back into the lungs.

A horse, on the other hand, if obliged to vomit, cannot completely cover the larynx, and so food regurgitates down its nostrils and may get into the lungs and cause pneumonia. Some horses compelled to vomit actually rupture their stomachs in the attempt.

Any animals capable of vomiting must possess a vomiting centre in the hinder part of the brain. This nerve centre controls and directs additional nerve centres which control the various muscles involved in the act of vomiting.

Working in the other direction, the reflex that induces vomiting is stimulated by impulses originating in various organs of the body which transmit messages to the vomiting centre in the brain and stir it to action. Such organs include the throat (pharynx), oesophagus, liver, intestine (particularly the small intestine), uterus, kidney, and even the brain itself, often through the semicircular canals contained within the middle ear. These are particularly involved in cases of motion sickness whether on land or water.

Vomiting, therefore, must not be regarded as a disturbance essentially confined to the digestive tract without full consideration of other possibilities. Vomiting may arise from kidney disorders (uraemic vomiting), from uterine disturbances as in early pregnancy and in cases of pyometra (pus in the uterus), travel sickness, and in rare cases from responses to particular odours or flavours.

Areca nut, ground and placed on the tongue—an old treatment for tapeworms—will frequently induce vomiting. so will a small piece of washing soda, as well as various emetic injections, which are absorbed into the blood and carried to the vomiting centre in the brain.

Motion sickness (car, train or boat) is due to the movements of fluid contained within the bony semicircular canals of the middle ear.

Intestinal disorders as a cause of vomiting may include poisons of various degrees of intensity, digestive upsets, particularly when bones have been chewed and swallowed.

In puppies intussusception (telescoping) of the bowel is a common cause. The vomiting is frequently repeated, often without the delivery of any material from stomach or bowel. Collapse is not far distant and only an early operation can be of help. Within 48 hours the bowel imprisoned in the telescoping will become gangrenous.

Any foreign body that blocks the intestine, usually the smaller section, will cause repeated vomiting. The object responsible may be a stone, a bone, a nut (of vegetable or mineral variety), a needle or a nail, a nylon stocking, a rubber ball (often a hollow ball, collapsed) and a great variety of other objects.

The presence of a foreign body in the intestine may usually be determined by palpation (fingers and thumb) or by X-ray examination. Many solid objects do not show up readily in a film, depending a great deal upon the amount of mineral substance they contain.

Foreign bodies in the stomach are more frequently those that can be swallowed and subsequently neither vomited up nor passed through the pylorus. Stockings come in this category, though some portion of one may pass down into the intestine. Flint, stones, and rubber balls are other examples.

Severe constipation, the accumulation of a quantity of finely chewed bone in the large intestine or rectum, may cause occasional vomiting with repeated unsuccessful attempts to effect a passage. String may protrude from the rectum but should never be pulled. Usually there is a ball of string or a large knot at the other end (occasionally a fish hook) and attempts to withdraw it will cause corrugation or intussusception of the intestine. If draughts of liquid paraffin do not permit the string to be passed, nothing remains but surgical operation.

Another rather uncommon cause of acute vomiting in the dog is a sudden, unexpected contact with a garden toad. The saliva of the toad is highly toxic, and even a drop carried on the creature's skin is enough to produce symptoms of vomiting and collapse in a susceptible dog. Usually recovery occurs within twelve hours provided the patient is kept warm and quiet.

Apart from the old emetic, washing soda, other chemicals used by the veterinary surgeon in an attempt to expel foreign bodies from the stomach are apomorphine given by injection, morphia, and large doses of salt and water by mouth.

The secret of success in most cases of vomiting due to

bowel obstruction from any cause whatever, is immediate operation. Delay can be fatal.

The Mechanism of Vomiting

Vomiting implies the spasmodic ejection of the contents of the stomach and sometimes of the intestine through the oesophagus and mouth.

The act has been divided into:

(*a*) Psychological vomiting, associated with unpleasant tastes or odours, fear or emotional disturbances.

(*b*) Physiological vomiting, which includes car and sea sickness, and the vomiting sometimes observed in bitches in early pregnancy. It might also include the vomiting seen in many bitches at about the sixth week following whelping when the mother vomits partly digested food, which the puppies devour. The vomiting present in cases of closed pyometra (pus in the uterus) may be included as another example. Vomiting resulting from the swallowing of indigestible materials may also be physiological.

(*c*) Pathological vomiting, associated with liver and kidney disease, enlarged spleen, virus infection, and inflammation of the stomach and intestine caused by bacterial infections and by food poisoning and by the ingestion of other toxic materials.

Not infrequently there may be overlapping of these three types. Vomiting has a great variety of causes and if it is repeated on more than two occasions it must never be treated lightly.

In many cases vomiting is beneficial, being Nature's way of relieving the effects of over-eating or of eating harmful or indigestible materials.

When an immovable foreign body is present in the bowel vomiting is actually harmful. In cases of inflamation of the stomach and/or intestines, repeated vomiting may deprive the body of fluid and cause dangerous dehydration which may have to be countered by the subcutaneous infiltration of normal saline solution.

When a dog is about to vomit, the brain centre is stimulated and transmits messages to the groups of muscles employed in the process. The pylorus, the valvular outlet from the stomach, closes, while the entrance to the stomach from the oesophagus relaxes.

The chest muscles next contract in order to fix the ribs, and the muscles of the abdominal wall undergo spasmodic (intermittent) contractions. The muscle wall of the oesophagus (food pipe) goes into what is known as retro-peristalis. In other words, instead of the muscular contractions running *down* the oesophagus, they go into reverse and run *upwards*. The glottis (soft palate) automatically closes over the opening of the larynx so that no food can be sucked into the lungs.

The abdominal muscles contract, and with the aid of a lowering of the pressure within the chest brought about by the muscular contraction holding the ribs in a fixed position, the contents of the stomach (and maybe of some of those of the small intestine) may be partly propelled, partly sucked into the oesophagus which, by reversing its contractions, carries the stomach contents into the mouth from which they are rapidly expelled.

Repeated vomiting may be accompanied by diarrhoea when the condition is caused by bacteria or a virus, also when an irritant poison has been swallowed. Vomiting with diarrhoea may occur in hepatitis infection and also in true distemper.

Another form of vomiting seen in puppies from an early age may be due to congenital constriction, and hardening of the wall of the pylorus, the outlet from the stomach. This responds to operative treatment.

Another variety comes from congenital stricture of the oesophagus. This is rapidly followed by dilation of the portion of the oesophagus immediately in front of the stricture.

A third variety in puppies and young dogs arises through the oesophagus within the thorax (chest) becoming imprisoned by an abnormal condition of one of the branches of the aorta. The oesophagus becomes squeezed within an arterial arch and a ligament holding the arch in position. This is also amenable to operation but in most cases where dilation of the oesophagus has already occurred the prospect is not encouraging.

In order to test for an oesophageal obstruction, either congenital or acquired as when a puppy (or older dog) swallows a lump of gristle, or a chop bone or a portion of one, offer it a few tiny pieces of meat, not larger than good-sized green peas. Usually they will be accepted. In about three minutes, if an obstruction exists, the dog will tuck its nose into its breast and make violent attempts to vomit. This may succeed in returning the fragments of meat but not in dislodging the foreign body. When this is in the upper part of the neck it may be felt, and a veterinary surgeon may be able to extract it or push it down into the stomach. Failing this he will open the oesophagus and remove it. Oesophageal wounds usually take some little while to heal.

If the foreign body lies in the thoracic portion of the oesophagus (beneath the ribs) and immediately below the backbone, the dog will be given a small barium meal, and its chest X-rayed. Alternatively, a plastic probang will be pushed down the oesophagus as far as it will go. The probang contains a metal ball at one end, which shows up very clearly in the film and discloses the position of the obstruction.

To effect its removal it is necessary to resect a rib. As the thorax is normally airtight and contains a potential vacuum, removal of a rib would be fatal unless it were possible to inflate the lungs at regular intervals, as occurs during normal breathing. This is done by inserting a tube into the trachea and making it a perfect fit by inflating its walls. A mixture of oxygen and an anaesthetic is then pumped into the lungs at normal breathing rate and maintained until the chest wound has been carefully sutured.

FITS

Fits take a variety of forms in dogs, just as in other animals. The general behaviour described as a fit involves salivation with champing movements of the jaws, usually followed by the sudden onset of spasmodic muscular contractions involving the head and neck, limbs and, possibly, other parts of the body, accompanied in many instances by interference with consciousness, partial or complete.

The duration of the fit may be a matter of seconds or minutes only, or the attacks may be repeated at intervals. Sometimes the condition persists for hours or days without any marked periods of remission. The severity of such fits may be so marked that they continue even when the dog is under anaesthesia.

The attacks may disappear and never return or they may recur after long or short intervals during puppyhood, sometimes with occasional appearances throughout the animal's life. Much depends upon whether the cause can be discovered and is capable of removal, or if it involves irreversible changes that have taken place in the brain.

Fits vary enormously in their pattern, but in individual cases accompanied by frequent repetition the pattern usually remains fairly constant so long as the cause is unchanged.

Although dogs of most or all breeds may develop fits, there are in some strains or families hereditary tendencies that may increase susceptibility. The type of temperament inherited may confer greater nervous sensitivity and a diminished capability to compete with the strains and stresses associated with domestication. This may account for some of the fits seen in quite young puppies, and it may be that they are born with a brain defect.

On the other hand, a simpler explanation may be that certain strains may be abnormally sensitive to the migration of worm (ascaris) larvae throughout their bodies and nervous mechanism. The primary infection may come through the dam.

The point of origin of a fit is situated actually within

the brain or its coverings (meninges), or it may arise from increased pressure of fluid present in one of the normal brain cavities. When the brain itself remains normal the fit is produced by abnormal outgoing impulses from the brain being transmitted to the muscles of the body under the influence of ingoing messages transmitted to the brain from some part of the body subjected to abnormal irritation. The local irritation responsible for such messages to the brain may be situated in the ears, in some portion of the alimentary tract, from the skin or the eyes, or in fact, from any part of the body.

Other causes of brain irritation include the presence of chemical substances within the blood. These may come from poison taken in through the mouth or injected into the animal, or may be associated with the presence of a toxin, or to excess or deficiency of some necessary hormone. Not uncommonly, a hormone imbalance gives rise to a corresponding mineral imbalance with alteration in the blood content of calcium, magnesium or phosphorus, or all three. Sometimes in diabetic subjects the fits may arise from imbalance between blood sugar and insulin.

In dogs of any age, but more usually in young dogs, especially those that have not been vaccinated against distemper, virus hepatitis and leptospiral jaundice, fits may be the first manifestation of an attack of one of these diseases already involving the brain cells. Conversely, the brain symptoms may never make their appearance or they may crop up weeks after apparent recovery from the primary infection.

Fits may occur during the course of kidney infections owing to accumulation of toxic products in the blood.

In heart conditions, particularly in older dogs, fainting attacks are sometimes accompanied by struggling, recurring at frequent intervals.

Lactation in bitches, resulting in a lowering of the calcium content of the blood may produce hypocalcaemic symptoms (milk fever), frequently including tetany (muscle stiffness) and convulsions.

Accidental injury to the brain during puppyhood, as from a fall upon the head, may cause fits immediately or at a later date, and in some instances these fits may occur at intervals throughout the animal's lifetime.

Teething, especially when changing the canine teeth, will sometimes produce fits in susceptible puppies. These usually disappear when the second teeth come down. Such fits may be confused with those produced by round worms, which frequently cause trouble at about this age. At teething time the administration of tablets containing calcium gluconate and vitamin D may be helpful.

Epilepsy

In a recent survey, Dr. Phyllis G. Croft discussed 260 cases of fits in dogs, and recorded electroencephalograms from each. From the results it was assumed that 167 of the 260 affected dogs examined were effected with epilepsy. The ages ranged from one to ten years, more often between one and three years. The incidence diminished from the fourth to the ninth years with a slight rise again at ten years. All the common breeds appear to have been represented.

Fits Associated with the Ears

The more characteristic symptom is the position of the head, drawn usually down on one side or lifted upwards and backwards. Apart from infection conveyed by ear mites, the possible presence of one or more rapidly burrowing barley grass awns must always be borne in mind.

Fits due to ear mites may be seen occasionally in puppies, only a few months old, that have obtained them from the ears of the mother.

Fits Associated with the Alimentary Tract

Overeating, especially at weaning age, may give rise to a

fit or fits, usually of short duration, if the puppy is fasted for some hours.

The need to worm puppies is always apparent but great care must be taken in the choice of a vermicide. Veterinary surgeons nowadays stock efficient remedies that produce no side-effects.

Fits Associated with the Skin

Heavy infestation with lice or fleas, and certain allergic skin irritations, have been suspected as being the cause of fits. It is probable that such symptoms arise only when there is an inborn predisposition to epilepsy.

Eyes and Fits

It has been recorded that some strains of puppies showing a tendency to fits are less susceptible if kept in the dark, possibly because they see less that is likely to disturb them.

Certain strains of puppies will develop fits if exposed to strong sunlight or when electric lights are turned on after dark. The probability is that these strains have an epileptic background.

Fits Caused by Chemicals

Chemical substances capable of producing fits or convulsive symptoms resembling them, include lead, derived from drinking water and bad plumbing; agene, formerly used in bleaching flour—a very serious cause of so-called 'hysteria' in dogs during and before the war years—and strychnine, which produces muscular contractions, followed by death.

Slug bait in the form of methaldehyde is commonly laid in gardens and is readily eaten by dogs and cats. In small doses it causes intoxication. Larger doses produce incoordination of limb movements, rapid breathing, muscular twitching, rapid movements of the eyeballs (nystagmus), followed by unconsciousness and heart failure. The hypodermic injection of apomorphine, followed by atropine, usually succeeds if the dose is not too large and the interval between ingestion and injection not too protracted.

16

A Dog in the Kennel

A kennel may contain any number of dogs simply because their owner is a fancier in the true sense of the word. On the other hand, the owner may be an optimist, interested in one or more breeds but hoping to make a profit out of his enterprise.

It must be said in favour of genuine fanciers that very few ever do make a profit out of dog breeding and exhibiting and yet the great majority remain fanciers all their lives. The pleasure they derive from their ceaseless efforts to breed dogs true to type and a little better than the other fellow's, more than compensates for the many sacrifices so many of them have to make in the pursuit of their hobby. Moreover, the amount of time they spend with their dogs gives them no opportunity to indulge in what might turn out to be even more extravagant forms of amusement, so in the long run what they lose on the swings they may possibly save on the roundabouts, and with a bit of luck they may manage to break even.

A minority, who maintain large kennels with a floating population, may be interested only in the commercial side of breeding, buying and selling dogs; the importance of the dog being entirely measured in terms of pounds, shillings, and pence. Others, who claim to have the financial interests of their country at heart, have helped to establish a considerable export trade in dogs, and it is to be hoped that they send them overseas with an easy conscience and an assurance that the dogs will not suffer in transit and will be happy and suitably appreciated by their new owners in a strange, foreign environment.

Kennels exist in a variety of forms and, like human abodes, vary from hovels to luxury homes provided with all modern conveniences. Certain basic features can be incorporated with advantage into every range of kennels, whatever their type. They should be wind- and water-tight so far as roofs and walls are concerned, with windows that, while giving sufficient light by day, can be partly opened with no fear of the inmates escaping.

All sleeping beds should have at least four inches open space between them and floor level. They should be provided with loose tops that can be lifted out to be scrubbed and disinfected.

Some means of providing additional warmth during four months of the year is essential, and this may be provided by the use of night-storage heaters with the addition of some infra-red heaters for puppies and whelping bitches and any possible invalids.

Wherever possible, an isolation quarter should be available not only in case of sickness but also for the safe keeping of young puppies prior to and after vaccination against distemper and other diseases. Separate feeding and cleansing utensils, brooms, pails, and barrows, should be reserved for the isolation quarter.

A good water supply is essential to ensure cleanliness. It is becoming more and more evident that soap and water are still the best safeguards against infection, and that so-called 'disinfectants' have little value against certain types of infectious diseases at the concentration it is safe to use where a number of dogs are already kennelled or where it is necessary to return dogs to their kennels shortly after their use. Formaldehyde, despite its unpleasant effects upon eyes and nose, used either in dilution or as a fumigant, is probably more generally effective against disease bacteria than some of the more modern preparations.

A building that can be rendered airtight, or nearly so, can be fumigated by mixing sufficient liquid formaldehyde with permanganate of potash crystals, the whole being contained in a clean, strong can, or, better still, in an old iron saucepan. This, with its contents, should be placed on a firm support three feet from the ground, and the doors and windows firmly closed for the ensuing twelve or twenty-four hours. The windows and doors will need to be left wide open for several hours longer before it will be safe to return the dogs to their kennels.

When there has been a contagious skin disease in a kennel it may be more satisfactory to substitute one of the old-fashioned sulphur candles for the formaldehyde, or to put a few red-hot ashes in the iron saucepan and throw upon them a few tablespoonsful of sulphur, taking all precautions against fire risk. The kennels are closed, as previously described, for twenty-four hours.

Electricity is generally available today where dogs are kept and great care must be taken to see that no leads are left in exposed positions where they can be chewed, with fatal results. Electric fires tend to be highly dangerous unless they are firmly attached to a non-inflammable wall, well out of reach of any of the occupants.

Oil heaters are too dangerous to be considered in kennels where they might get knocked over, or liberate fumes. Properly spaced infra-red lamps are good, provided they are hung well above sleeping places, but they are capable, even at temperatures that can be borne, of causing serious skin burns in sleeping dogs and puppies exposed too long to their influence. It is advisable to hang them above one end of a bed or sleeping place so that the occupants can move away from the main source of heat, remembering always that the maximum heat available should not be sufficient to cause burns.

Bedding

The choice of suitable material can be a problem. Wood-wool entangles limbs; straw, hay, and sawdust favour the presence and multiplication of fleas, lice, and other parasites. So do rugs, blankets, and all kinds of cloth.

A machine is available for cutting old newspapers into short, thin strips, or it can be torn by hand, but takes time. Paper has the advantage that it can be taken out and burnt without undue smoke or smell. Old newspapers can be bought very cheaply and occupy little space when folded.

For whelping bitches a bed of newspaper strips can be covered by an untorn complete paper, which provides a very safe surface.

Exercise

Dogs of all sizes and breeds require daily exercise but the healthy gundog or terrier, to take an example, is capable of walking many more miles than its owner.

Walks take up a great deal of the dog owner's time but they have the advantage that they get the dogs away from grassland and on to the hard roads, which are good for limbs, pasterns, and feet. Grass is taboo as it induces flat feet and slack pasterns and prevents proper muscular development.

Hard, rough tracks are best where available. Very few bad feet and pasterns are seen among cattle, dogs and the like on the hills. Those who live near the coast, where hard, flat sandy stretches are available at low tide, are fortunate. Today, the bicycle with a string of dogs following it along a rough country road is a thing of the past and would certainly be a poor insurance risk.

Although an occasional gallop may do no harm, especially to greyhounds and the gundogs, walking on a lead is usually the better method in dogs preparing for exhibition. It produces firm muscle without overloading the shoulders, and is particularly valuable for strengthening forearms and second thighs. It keeps elbows tight and in place and, in addition, it lessens the likelihood of accidental injury.

Every kennel should have some means of weighing the dogs, to determine the weight at which every dog in the kennel is at its optimum degree of fitness; a little adjustment of the rations will keep it at that weight.

Refrain from converting the dog's interior into a medicine chest since animals that are properly cared for, fed, and exercised, need very little medicine, except in states of emergency, apart from early worming and vaccination against all the diseases to which they may become susceptible in later life as the result of infection. All these can now be combined in a single injection.

When health problems arise the dog owner will do well to consult a veterinary surgeon rather than seek friendly advice elsewhere.

17

A Dog in the Home

There are two important occasions in the life of every man. The first is when he brings a wife into the home; the second is when he acquires a dog. It is to be hoped that the three will accept one another with grace and true affection to form a trinity, a partnership mutually agreeable to all parties.

Taking a dog into the house, whatever the domestic situation, is indeed a serious step and one that nobody, man or woman, should take without very serious consideration. Once the decision to do so has been taken, the dog must be accepted as a member of the family, to receive and return affection while its life shall last. To the uninitiated this may appear to be a sentimental or even an unhealthy way of regarding a four-legged member of a human household, but all of us who have owned and loved dogs over a period of many years will agree that sentiment is quite unavoidable in one's relationship with a dog just as it is in one's relationship with the other members of the family.

Only a veterinary surgeon in constant touch with numerous households, their owners, their children and their dogs, can fully understand how vital a part the dog plays in the family life and what a gap is manifest whenever through accident or illness the dog is taken from them.

Those to whom the presence or the absence of a dog means little or nothing should never contemplate taking one into the home. An unfortunate fact, too, is that in favourable circumstances the life of a dog seldom averages more than a dozen years while its owner may reasonably hope to attain three score and ten. The consequence is that the confirmed dog lover may experience as many as six heartbreaks. Against this, one must take into consideration the years one may enjoy and share with each dog as a companion.

When circumstances permit, it is better always to own two dogs. One is company for the other, and if there happens to be some disparity in their respective ages it is less likely that you will be left entirely without a dog in the home, and that you will be able to replace the departed with another dog, younger than the one left behind.

In many respects dogs resemble children. Both start very much in the same way, but how they develop depends greatly upon the manner in which they are brought up and how they are taught to behave. Parents are usually responsible for their child's manners and the owner for those of his dog, provided that he has owned it from puppyhood. How it was treated between the 10th and 14th weeks of its life will be reflected in its behaviour thereafter.

It is always wise to acquire a puppy at about eight weeks of age, when first it is removed from its mother, and for the next two or three months its training as far as possible should be undertaken by one person, preferably by the one who will be most closely associated with its daily life and routine. You must be firm, kind and very patient, and also quite certain what you want the puppy to do and how to communicate this to the puppy mind. If the puppy prefers its natural behaviour to that more generally approved by human society, it will be patience and persistence that will win the day, whether it is that of the pupil or the teacher.

Animals do not learn through punishment as children are supposed to do, since children are better able to distinguish between what their elders consider right and wrong, and they have a better understanding of cause and effect. As it cannot talk or understand (as yet) the meaning of words and human expression, a puppy does not know what one wants it to do, or why it is punished for doing something which, to the mind of the puppy, is perfectly natural.

As soon as it is fixed in its mind that soiling the drawing room carpet is wrong by human standards and that it must make an effort to get out into the garden when nature calls, it will show some willingness to co-operate.

If it now really knows what is expected from it in the

way of behaviour and flatly refuses to comply, either from laziness or lack of respect for the dictates of humanity, a mild reproof is justifiable, and very soon the puppy will begin to learn that disobedience brings retribution.

The need to instil into the puppy mind just what it is that its owner desires it to do, applies as much in the drawing room as in the field, the showring, or even in the circus. Once get it into the dog's mind what is required of it and usually it will be quite willing to play the part provided always that it is asked to do something it likes to do, feels under some obligation to obey, or regards the whole performance as some kind of a game. Most dogs are very appreciative of applause, just as they hate ridicule, and they will act a part over and over again in the circus so long as the audience will continue to clap and cheer.

They also appreciate some small reward for good behaviour. It may be a sweet or a meaty tit-bit. A puppy or a dog can be persuaded to do most things it is capable of doing if this recipe is adopted:

Cut a small piece of liver into thin slices and fry them lightly in butter. Take them out of the pan while hot and let them cool on a plate. Cut the cold liver into small dice, and carry some in the pocket, contained in a purse or a plastic bag. Practically all dogs are susceptible to bribery and will answer the call of anyone willing to provide small pieces of delectable liver in return for services rendered. The same dog would give a wide berth to any person who attempted to train it whip-in-hand.

It is fatal to scold a dog that runs away, and to chase after it. It is equally so to scold or whip it when it is caught. The right thing to do, especially when armed with the bag of liver, is to turn round and walk away in the opposite direction. Finding itself deserted the puppy will alter course and begin to follow. This is the moment to produce the liver, and having enticed it to hand give it several pieces as a reward. Always train a puppy on an empty stomach and feed it after the lesson is over. Be patient at all times, and never lose your temper or raise your voice, except when in response to wilful disobedience—not then, if you can avoid it.

Always keep a light, round collar on your dog, fitted with name, address and phone number, for the dog that is run over is very frequently one that slipped out when somebody came to the door. Teach your dog to walk on the lead always on the pavement, except at authorised crossing places. Never let it off the lead in public places even at night when traffic is almost absent. A great many dogs coming into the veterinary surgery at night are brought from quiet roads. The usual explanation is: 'A car came suddenly round the corner. I've never seen a car there at night before!'

Bring your dog up not to be a nuisance by jumping up to callers and persons who speak to you in shops or on the pavement. If the dog is one that demands attention, teach it to sit in begging position rather than jump up and paw people's clothes with dirty feet.

Never feed it at table while you are having your own meal. If it makes you uncomfortable to eat without giving the dog a share, let it have something in a separate dish, that and no more.

All dogs love to have a chair of their own, which is far better than letting them occupy every chair in the house and leave them coated in short hairs, if your dog has that kind of coat. Label the back of the chair legibly with the dog's name (Fig. 11). The dog cannot read, but visitors can and will not plump themselves down in the chair and rise covered with hairs. Most dogs prefer to sleep in the chair at night rather than in a basket. If so, drop a piece of blanket over your dog before you retire for the night, except in summer. Do this after turning off the electric fire or putting a guard in front of an open grate. Never leave a coal fire open. The dog may jump out of bed with a piece of blanket still over its back. Many fires have started in this way. Dogs have also been frequently known to chew electric leads when bored by being left alone. This can be fatal, as well as another possible cause of fire.

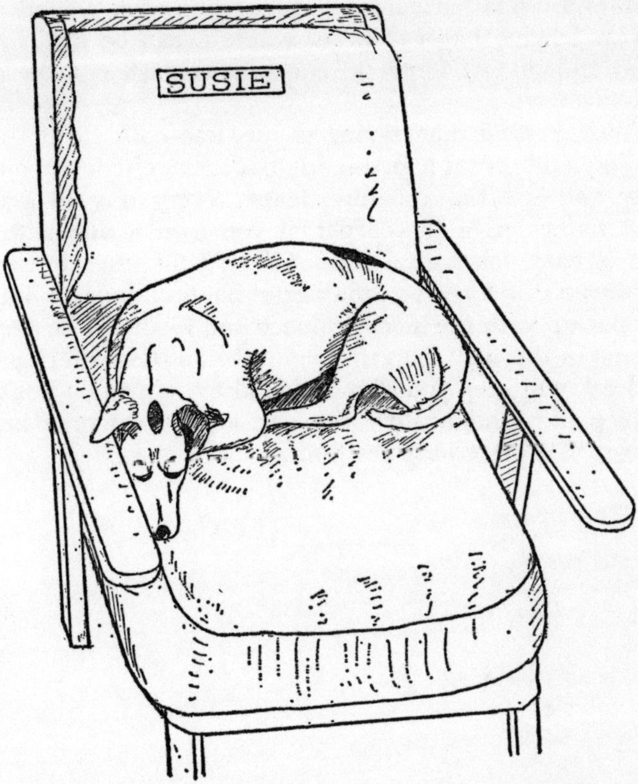

Figure 11 Label the back of the chair legibly with the dog's name

Never throw stones for your dog to chase and possibly retrieve, or sooner or later it will swallow one, and probably need an operation. This also applies to rubber balls, which when punctured sometimes collapse and are swallowed. Rubber bones and many doggy toys are equally dangerous.

If you feed bones to your dog let them be large marrow bones, uncooked. Never on any account give it chop bones or bones from poultry. Feed your dog its main meal at night and half an hour later take it for its walk. There is a close relationship between feeding time and bowel movement and the latter is most frequent soon after a good meal. Always leave a basin of water where it can be found at all times and do not forget to empty and wash out the basin daily.

You may find that having to buy and cook meat, groom the dog, and give it a fortnightly bath, exercise it three times daily and use the vacuum cleaner every day to get the short hairs out of the carpet, if you own a dog with this kind of coat, takes up a good deal of your time, but if you are a true dog lover you may grumble occasionally but you will put up with the inconvenience and labour. The exercise you get in this way, plus that you take on the owner's end of the lead, will keep you slim and healthy. If you do not want to keep slim and healthy you can keep a cat or a budgie instead, but preferably not both.

Index